The F Word: Global Issues That Unite
the Feminist Movement

Amya Gulati

THE
F WORD:
GLOBAL
ISSUES
THAT
UNITE THE
FEMINIST
MOVEMENT

AMYA GULATI

NEW DEGREE PRESS

COPYRIGHT © 2020 AMYA GULATI

THE F WORD: GLOBAL ISSUES THAT UNITE THE FEMINIST
MOVEMENT

ISBN   978-1-64137-907-6 *Paperback*

         978-1-64137-643-3 *Kindle Ebook*

         978-1-64137-645-7 *Ebook*

"Fight for the things that you care about, but do it in a way that will lead others to join you."

—RUTH BADER GINSBURG

CONTENTS

To my family, for loving and supporting me unconditionally.

To Neha, for staying true to your beliefs
and inspiring me to do the same.

And to Caelan, for always being right by my side.

PROLOGUE

———

"You know how I'm horrible at physics?" my friend said.

"You're not that bad," I lied. The girl was pulling straight D's.

"Well my parents had a parent-teacher conference the other day with my physics teacher, and my dad said the most sexist shit in the world when they were talking about my grades."

Her father asked her physics teacher if she might not be getting good grades in the class because she was a girl. Her physics teacher looked at her father, confused and slightly taken aback by the question. He told her father that some of his best students are girls; her gender had nothing to do with it. No one's good at everything, so physics probably isn't her strongest suit.

"Why did my dad have to bring my gender into it?" My friend shook her head and then never talked to me about it again. I think about it now and then, and it makes my blood boil every time.

Feminism is such a complex topic. A stigma exists suggesting it's not really about equality—that people who claim to be feminists are really just trying to prove they are better than men or superior to the other gender. It suggests when women talk about the everyday issues they face simply due to their gender, they're making it up because they want attention, hate all men, or are angry and crazy.

Often times, I think about how fortunate I am to be living in America. By law, women can do everything men can do. No explicit law exists restricting women from having the same jobs as men, going out late at night by themselves, or letting their voices be heard outside their homes. But even with these basic rights, women still don't earn the same money on the dollar, they walk in fear of being attacked as the sun sets, and they're often shunned by society for speaking out in the same manner as men.

People still embrace stereotypes deeply integrated into our society that seek to keep women on a lower platform than men. People still believe women can't do math and science, they are less than their husbands, and they can't make decisions for themselves. Women and men do not have it the same. This is not an opinion; it is a fact. It is an unfortunate reality that makes women turn to feminism, and it's the reason why some men and women regard feminism as an angry cult of crazy women.

Many believe that equality has already been achieved. In their minds, the right to vote and the right to join the workforce was all equality really entailed. Others do not believe in equality. Men and women just aren't the same because our biology makes us different. So what the hell are these feminists even fighting for?

By definition, Feminism is "the belief in the social, economic, and political equality of the sexes."[1] Modern feminism in a country like America has less to do with governmental or legal issues than with our societal structure and the way our culture does not permit women and men to be perceived as equal. Businesses have found loopholes in paying women less than men for working the same jobs. Corporations are structured in such a way that the government has little say in their workings, hiring, or pay process, so when it comes down to the paycheck, women see less zeros than men. On top of that, when women are raped or assaulted in America, it isn't uncommon for some to wonder what the woman did to deserve it. Was she out too late at night? Was she intoxicated? What was she wearing? Was she, god forbid, by herself?

While in a discussion about rape, someone once said to me, "You can't expect to leave your doors unlocked and not have something stolen." In case you weren't able to decipher this incredibly fucked up analogy, "the house" in this case is a woman, and leaving the "door unlocked" has to do with a woman putting herself in a "sticky situation." The analogy the speaker used essentially states this hypothetical—but oftentimes real—woman was asking for it.

This type of overt sexism can be seen in many instances. An assertive man is confident and knows what he is doing,

---

1   *Encyclopedia Britannica Online*, Academic ed., s.v. "Feminism," accessed April 28, 2020.

whereas an assertive woman is a bitch. She's just trying to feel good about herself by bringing other people down. Our society is built on the stereotype that a female must maintain a certain number of feminine qualities, including being quiet, doing as she is told, and not saying exactly what she means to avoid hurting anyone else's feelings.

Women deal with some form of sexism on a regular basis, whether it be from their partners, the companies they work for, or their own fathers. My friend had a rude awakening that day—just like most women do at some point in their lives—that she would be treated very differently if she was a boy.

***

This book will cover global issues beyond common knowledge. Some things in this book I had no awareness of until I researched deeper into global feminism. I did my best to cover major countries and cultures around the world, but of course, I was unable to cover everything. *The F Word* could be the first in a series of books on feminism, and I will continue to bright light every injustice until the doctors tell me I have carpal tunnel and can no longer write.

I'm writing this book to tell you how it feels to be a woman. I'm writing this book to tell you that there are so many obstacles women must overcome every day but do not share with the rest of the world. I'm writing this book because I feel for other women in other countries and societies who have it so much worse than I do. I'm writing this book because I used to be so afraid of speaking my mind due to the fear that people would so easily dismiss my thoughts.

I can't tell you how many times I have considered throwing the whole book away and writing about something else. I have thought about all the people that would just look at the cover and put the book back in disgust. I have wondered how many people will hate what I have to say and use their words to put my book to shame. I have had to remind myself I need to write this book, and if I don't, I will never truly be at peace.

This topic is controversial as hell, and there is no way to maneuver around feminism without offending at least half of the world's people. But some things aren't meant to be agreeable and pleasant. We need to talk about the things that make us uncomfortable, and this is one of those things for me. The fear I have of publishing this book is not enough to make me switch topics or hold back on my thoughts. I will speak my whole truth, and you are allowed to make whatever judgments or comments you so please. My only request to you, the reader, is to read the entirety of the book before making your assumptions on the topic or movement as a whole. Feminism, like I said earlier, is a multiplex subject that takes a fair amount of time to process and understand. I, myself, am still learning new things about this certain issue every day. I ask that you think beyond yourself and the people you know when making comparisons to the women in this book because everyone is dealing with their own set of demons.

PART I

CHAPTER ONE

CONSTRUCTION OF GENDER

———

Our world is constructed around gender. You can't escape it. If you take a step back and observe your environment, you will notice almost everything is assigned a gender. Blue means male, pink means female, bathrooms are separated into "women" and "men," and clothing stores are divided in half.

There are two arguments when it comes to gender, the first one being it is something you are born with, and the second being gender is created by us humans. While one could argue for either position, it's important to understand the history behind the former theory, as it is widely accepted by most of the world.

Most people would agree every human is born with their gender already assigned to them. Our biology is responsible for carving a path in our destiny, and our reproductive anatomy dictates our future. Men are from Mars, women are from

Jupiter, or something like that. Because men are born with more testosterone, an average of seven to eight times more than women, they also have more body hair, more muscle mass, and a deeper voice.[2] Women carry estrogen, which results in less body hair, higher body fat in certain areas, and a higher pitched voice. This is basic biology that, on its own, is just simple facts with little meaning. But when these scientific findings are applied to human behaviors, they lead to stronger, more insidious beliefs that have shaped today's society.

Testosterone plays a large factor in the growth of the testicles and penis. When a child goes through puberty, their body begins to produce a constant stream of testosterone, which further encourages the growth of the genitals, body hair, muscle size, and strength.[3] During this stage, there is also a notable increase in their libido.[4] These are innate biological processes that differentiate those that carry larger doses of testosterone and those that do not. The issue arises when these facts are misconstrued to aggregate the reasoning men are supposed to be sexually promiscuous, are physically superior and therefore more capable, and less emotionally unstable. Estrogen, on the other hand, tends to make women more irrational and less physically capable. Women are intended to be monogamists because of their low sex drive, and become emotionally attached to their sexual partners at a faster rate.

2   George Krucik, "The Effects of Testosterone on the Body," *Healthline,* September 17, 2018.

3   "Testosterone—What it Does and Doesn't Do," *Harvard Health Publishing,* August 29, 2019.

4   Ibid.

Therefore, because of such polar differences, men become great physical caretakers for the opposite sex while women excel in nurturing under stable environments. This thinking formed traditional gender roles and created a society that categorized all humans at birth as dominant or submissive, strong or weak, and master or servant.

Before I continue, I would like to reiterate the argument I am making does not pertain to debunking biology or science. I am examining the societal interpretation of scientific facts that oftentimes leave room for fallacies and bias. The theory that gender is present from birth is no exception.

I remember reading about phrenology for the first time in a psychology class. Its inaccurate findings were used to formulate theories on human behavior. Phrenology is a pseudoscience that became widely popular in the nineteenth and twentieth centuries. It observed the human skull and used measurements and structure to determine the mental and physical traits of a certain individual.[5] It was widely accepted as evidence based science until it was later debunked in the nineteenth century. However, the theory prevailed for centuries, and its principles have reigning influence over biological theories.

When studying women's skulls in comparison to men's, phrenologists noticed they were smaller by an average of five centimeters and were quick to come to the conclusion

5   *Encyclopaedia Britannica Online*, Academic ed., s.v. "Phrenology" accessed April 28, 2020.

women are less intelligent and have a lower mental capacity.[6] This assumption guided people to believe that *biologically* women are inferior, and this led to the furtherance of strict gender roles that kept women in the kitchen and men in the office. Scientists also found that different shaped skulls between Anglo-Saxons and African people insinuated the natural social hierarchy between the colonizer and the colonized, enforcing the white man's burden, or the belief that colored people are meant to be enslaved by Caucasian men.[7] Theories are susceptible to flaws, and it takes time, research, and further studies to expose them.

The misconstrued beliefs that women need saving and are biologically inferior is not only detrimental to a woman's image in society, but it has serious repercussions on the male as well. In the eighteenth and nineteenth centuries, men were expected to dress in suits and grow out their facial hair, following similar social constructs that females were forced to follow as well. Violent displays of manliness were key to many cultures' theories of true masculinity. Today's cultural norms have developed to accord with our society, but remain inimical nonetheless.

Because men are considered the stronger sex, they are expected to conceal their emotions to maintain the "tough guy" image. When men cry or express pain, they are ridiculed for being "pussies" and "weak" and are then told to "grow some balls." Studies show men are more likely to fall

---

6   Oliver G. Alvar. "The Disproven Theory That Was Used to Justify Racism and Sexism," *Cultura Colectiva*, October 19, 2018.

7   Ibid.

into depression, recover at a much slower rate, and consequentially, are also more likely to commit suicide. Recent research shows men are three times as likely to die by suicide than women. White men account for nearly 70 percent of yearly suicides.[8] This belief that men do not, or rather should not, show emotions has been instilled into the minds of humans from a very young age, and it is unfortunately something that resides with many for their entire life.

The notion that gender is made may not resound with those that strongly reside with the human application of biological findings. This argument insists certain institutions—family, education, marriage, and culture—express and normalize differences in gender roles, and it is not until a human is introduced to these institutions that they are forced to identify with a gender.

Cordelia Fine, a British psychologist and philosopher, is one of many researchers to argue scientific theories based on gender are flawed and debased with assumptions. In her book, *Delusions of Gender: The Real Science Behind Sex Differences*, she writes about the faint line between culture and gender.

"The social context influence s who you are, how you think and what you do,"

CORDELIA FINE SAYS.[9]

8   Stephen Rodrick, "All-American Despair," *Rolling Stone*, May 30, 2019.

9   Cordelia Fine, *Delusions of Gender: The Real Science Behind Sex Differences* (New York City: W.W. Norton & Company, 2010), 28.

Essentially, before humans even get to form an opinion on their identities, they are brought into a world that does that for them with a set of gender salient rules. Instead of considering ourselves in the context of *human*, we begin to think of ourselves in terms of our gender and the stereotypes that run alongside them. Humans have created the concept of gender at conception. It is not merely anything more than a social construct designed to segregate and differentiate humans, creating a society that enforces roles based on nothing more than the body parts one was born with. After all, you can't be what you can't see.

Now that I have thrown some terminology and theories into the air, I want to talk about my main issue with the construction of gender. I find that humans are introduced to gender from the day we are born, and that is what results in not just gender roles, but identity crisis as well. We are told to discover our interest among a list of options. If our interests fall outside the box, we become confused because that's not what we are told is "normal." We begin questioning ourselves and fearing we are not "normal." What really is the norm, if not conformity to act and behave like everyone else?

These theories are complex and even I find it difficult to strongly reside with the latter. However, I think questioning what we've always been told is right and the way things are is an essential part of establishing one's identity. I find the argument that "women and men are not equal, just different" somehow always relates back to biology and "the way we were born," but I've noticed that this statement often allows for many sexist and outdated concepts to go unnoticed. What is the difference between defending scientifically proven facts and the historical applications of them? When does it just become an excuse to continue to play out socially constructed gender roles that date back to the days when the average human couldn't read or write? No right or wrong answer exists. But there is no reason to accept all things for being the way they are without considering all of the surrounding theories and possibilities. *Question the norm.*

Unarguably, the acceptance and credence of gender inequality centuries ago established gender roles and societal expectations. In America, women were expected to look after the household while men went out to work. There was an emphasis on family life and wealth. This all unraveled with the rise of first-wave feminism—when white women demanded the right to vote and be included in political matters. Alongside women's suffrage was womanism, a movement that is still very much alive and present today, something we'll be talking about in later chapters.

CHAPTER TWO

WOMANISM

The traditional feminism movement disregarded women of color almost entirely, bringing suffrage rights strictly to white women and failing to mention the injustices colored women were regularly subjected to. An abundance of proof exists pointing to racist first wave feminist leaders who, not only adamantly refused to allow black women into their movement, but also advocated for the sterilization of minority women.

Women of color are double minorities, facing the challenges of not only being female but also nonwhite. The 1920s were rampant with racism particularly in the form of segregation, and feminism at this time was just another exclusionary movement further marginalizing colored women. For these reasons, minority women simply could not call themselves feminists.

Alice Walker describes a womanist as a woman of color who has a love for other women. As the term suggests, a womanist is an advocate for women. She has an admiration for other women's cultures, their nature, and their strengths.[10] A womanist is a "universalist" who does not regard one gender over the other; rather, she is committed to the "wholeness" of all of humanity in bringing the genders closer together.[11]

Black women took on womanism and fought not only for gender equality but against racial oppression on African women and men as well. While it is not a movement opposing traditional feminism, womanism can be seen as a furtherance of feminism that takes into account the disparities women of all races, ethnicities, and cultures endure while observing the intersectionality of these issues.

This is not to say what the feminists achieved in the 1920s was invalid or insignificant, but rather point to the fact that even revolutionary social movements come with their set of injustices and malpractices. In the United States, women, regardless of race, were bombarded with all kinds of social, political, and economic restrictions. They could not possess property under their name, receive a higher education beyond the secondary level, or vote in political elections. Domestic violence was normalized and encouraged while marital rape was not recognized as a criminal offense. Women received less money on the dollar (a present-day practice), and had absolutely no say in the regulation of their reproductive organs (an issue that is still being battled over). Women, regardless of the color of their skin, were second-class citizens in their own country.

---

10 Camille Rahatt, "How Alice Walker Created Womanism—The Movement That Meets Black Women Where Feminism Misses the Mark," *Blavity*, February 4, 2020.

11 Ibid.

The Second Great Awakening gave birth to the social reform movement of the nineteenth and twentieth centuries.[12] A wave of religious revival brought Christianity to American homes and encouraged women to become more actively involved in spreading moral values, such as motherhood and familialism, to others. Women began to obtain roles as moral advocates—an essential measure in the expansion of white women's rights—and found a community of like-minded individuals who shared a common goal: gender equality. It is important to point out that this religious reform was imposed on the middle and upper classes. The so-called "American Dream" and all of the social norms that followed it, didn't have regard for the lower class or people of color. Women of color were still expected to give birth, raise multiple children and do household work, all while working a low-pay job with little to no healthcare benefits.

The Seneca Falls Convention of 1844, what many consider to be the turning point in the feminist movement, was the first time a large group of women came together to discuss the changes they wished to see in regards to the treatment of women in society.[13] While the main topic of discussion was suffrage, the sessions were held by and pertained to the general issues of middle and upper-class white women. One of the main organizers of the convention, a name that many people have familiarized themselves with in regards to the feminist movement, Elizabeth Cady Stanton, made sure white

12   "The Second Great Awakening," *Lumen*, accessed May 7, 2020.

13   "Seneca Falls Convention," *Encyclopedia Britannica*, accessed May 7, 2020.

women were prioritized in the movement.[14] While Stanton was one of the first few recognized women who spoke outright in the suffrage movement, history books and school lessons fail to mention her abhorrent racism and classism.

According to Stanton, black men were not worthy of the right to vote, as they were all vile rapists and a threat to the white woman. "What will we and our daughters suffer if these degraded black men are allowed to have the rights that would make them even worse than our Saxon fathers?" She asks her fellow white suffragettes.[15] She believed the black man's suffrage would lead to the further debasing of white women in America, while maintaining a complete disregard for their equally significant counterpart: black women.

However, Stanton was not the only suffragette to make such polluted statements. Susan B. Anthony, Lucretia Mott, and several other white feminists during this time refused to include black Americans in their agenda. To put this exact disregard into perspective, Anthony was once noted saying that "she would sooner cut off her right arm before she would ever work for or demand the ballot for the black man and not the woman."[16]

---

14   "Seneca Falls Convention," *Encyclopedia Britannica*, accessed May 7, 2020.

15   Debra J. Dickerson, "Elizabeth Cady Stanton: Abolitionist, Founding Feminist and (yawn) Hypocrite," *Slate*, July 13, 2011.

16   Corrine Segal, "Hundreds of 'I Voted' Stickers Left at Susan B. Anthony's Grave," *PBS*, November 8, 2016.

How could a black woman feel safe in this movement? How would she be able to call the white women in this movement her "sisters?" Would a black woman's sister ever call her brother a rapist, simply for the color of his skin?

With present day as proof, the first-wave feminism movement was successful, and all women were given the right to vote in 1920. While the nineteenth amendment does not specify race, therefore enfranchising women of all color, white feminists cannot be credited for black suffrage. Stanton and Anthony did not invite black women to their meetings, did not want them to speak publicly or maintain a stance on black suffrage, and refused to convey their concerns to their larger audience. While black women sought to bring the right to vote for their entire community, including black men and white women, white feminists refused to expand their motives beyond white women.

Many black women acknowledge the modern feminist movement and applaud its achievements in today's society, but they point to the general disregard of the experiences and struggles of individual groups of women. Whether it be women of color, lesbian women, or indigenous women, oftentimes mainstream feminism looks to place struggles and goals of these groups under one umbrella. That simply cannot be done. The intersections between race and gender and sexuality and gender are tightly woven together, and one cannot fight for the equality of these women without fighting for other injustices. This is something first-wave feminists clearly did not come to terms with at the time, therefore bringing rise to womanism—an inclusive fight for equality recognizing the bond between the color of your skin and the gender you identify with—and working to abolish the stigma behind both of those factors simultaneously.

Now, imagine how much more powerful the movement would have been if white women were willing to work alongside black women. Imagine how much sooner the legislation would have passed if the movement had tripled in size with the inclusion of black women and men.[17] Black women, on their own, had less potential to make significant progress due to their double minority status, but had white women remained inclusionary, their joint crusade would be unstoppable.

This is a part of history you won't find in a lot of textbooks, novels, or websites. For that reason, many people unfortunately reside in the notion that first-wave feminism was inclusionary and righteous because, after all, the movement resulted in the twenty-first amendment, which gave white and black women the right to vote. Therefore, many womanists and modern-day feminists refuse to acknowledge the "accomplishments" of feminists during this time as their work was not truly revolutionary for all.

<hr />

17   Jerica Deck, "Why the Fight for Women's Rights Must Include Women of Color," *Global Citizen,* January 25, 2019.

CHAPTER THREE

WOMEN OF COLOR
IN AMERICA

———

Women, under many societal structures in various different countries, are treated as second-class citizens. The United States, while being one of the most opportunistic places for women and people of color, has yet to call itself a land that provides liberty and justice for all.

A nation that has worked hard to stray from its foundational roots built on racism and sexism, the US, still has a long way to go. As we all know, America truly belonged to the indigenous Native Americans until Christopher Columbus steered hundreds of thousands of miles in the wrong direction and decided to label a colored group of people "Indians," believing he had found the land of spices and gold. I'm not going to turn this book into a US history textbook but it is important to remember racism that was once embedded into a society will never truly vanquish centuries later. The same goes for sexism, women in all ethnic and racial groups during that time period—the 1600s and beyond—had fewer rights than their male counterparts and this can be seen in the very laws of every society today.

During the era of slavery and segregation, African American women were living in their own personal hell. While being subject to punishment, cruelty, and the common mistreatment all blacks faced, black women in particular faced their own set of issues, which included rape, assault, and unwanted pregnancies. Many female slaves were taken advantage of by their male owners and were unaware of the life growing inside them. Due to the time period and their horrible living conditions (if you can even call it living), many black women had brutal miscarriages and lost their jobs, as well as access to the little resources they had. Some women were also beaten by the man who had forced themselves on them until a miscarriage transpired. Those that had delivered children were banished or even murdered by their female owners upon learning about their cheating husbands. Black women were subject to a level of cruelty no man had or could have ever endured.

Today, many black women are lawyers, doctors, entrepreneurs, musical artists, and live the healthy and happy life they were denied just a century ago. These successful African American women went to public high schools, most likely attended college, and raised their families they had always dreamed of having. Unfortunately, that cannot be said for all black women. Many of which are still stuck in a cycle of poverty that continues to destroy families, corrupt young children, and prevent young adults from having successful careers. It is a concept called systemic inequality, and it is the reason we still have ghettos and slums in some of the biggest and brightest cities in America.

Studies show black American incomes and financial stability have been increasing over time, but those numbers are minuscule and are flailing compared to the increasing values of white Americans. This is due to policies that are specifically targeted against African Americans. For example, the very structure of "black neighborhoods" differs to white neighborhoods. They have fewer resources available to them, including fewer hospitals and subpar health services, with black mothers and their children dying at higher disproportionate rates than their white counterparts.[18] Another issue that receives the hot spot in political debates from time to time is gerrymandering, or the manipulation of electoral boundaries that is used to favor one party, race, and/or class.[19] Gerrymandering has consistently ensured African Americans are rarely, if ever, represented by candidates that have their best interests in mind. Majority-minority districts concentrate their minority vote in highlighted districts, reducing Democratic influence in all other districts.[20] This method of packing minorities into a couple districts may seem as though it is handing over political influence to colored communities, but it is actually giving as much power to the opposing party as possible. Because both the Democratic and

18 Jamila Taylor, Cristina Novoa, Katie Hamm, and Shilpa Phadke, "Eliminating Racial Disparities in Maternal and Infant Mortality," *Center for American Progress,* May 2, 2019.

19 Olga Pierce and Kate Rabinowitz, "'Partisan' Gerrymandering Is Still About Race," *ProPublica,* October 9, 2017.

20 Ibid.

Republican parties follow this practice, it has been difficult for lawmakers, congress people, and citizens opposed to the practice to make gerrymandering an invalid process. These are just a few issues the black community faces as a whole, but black women today have their own set of battles as well.

Black women have risen from their history and joined the workforce in a number of different jobs and industries, and while they may go out and get the highest degree possible and the best job in their city, a massive pay gap is still enforced through racial and gender bias. The average black woman earns sixty-one cents for every dollar earned by a white man, which means in one year, she will make $23,653 less than her male counterpart.[21] To really drive that statistic home, this $23,653 amounts to $946,120 in the span of a forty-year career.[22]

The same can be said about Hispanic, Asian (East and South), and Pacific Islander women. Latina women are paid 46 percent less than white men and 31 percent less than white women.[23] These numbers apply to Latina women holding the same jobs as white men; for example, Latina nurses are making an annual salary of about $56,700 while white men make about $69,000, creating an 18 percent gap in just this one field.[24] Point being, the positions and work being done is equivalent while the pay is not. Asian American and Pacific

---

21 Sarah O'Brien, "Here's How the Wage Gap Affects Black Women," *CNBC*, August 22, 2019.

22 Ibid.

23 "The Latina Pay Gap by the Numbers," Lean In, accessed May 8, 2020.

24 Ibid.

Islander women who work full-time and maintain yearly jobs make eighty-five cents for every dollar than the average white man.[25] This gap extends when comparing women to their male counterparts within the same racial group: Asian American women earn seventy-six cents for every dollar Asian American men make.[26] These numbers might not seem alarming on paper, but they add up and create huge disparities in comparative annual salaries.

Prior to the twenty-first century, legal restrictions were pragmatically used to exclude all women—regardless of their race or ethnicity—from many high-paying jobs reserved exclusively for men. While white women were slowly allowed into the same work fields as men over time, women of color were continually looked down on and were given the shorter end of the stick when it came to working the higher salary jobs. Even when they hold jobs traditionally held by men or white workers, especially managerial and leadership roles, black women often encounter discrimination and resistance due to their race and gender. Typical stereotypes and traditional outlooks label them as "bitchy," "lazy," and "scary," terms that most women, regardless of the color of their skin, have been labeled from their male co-workers. Even words like "honey," "sweetheart," and "darling" are often used to belittle female employees and make them feel uncomfortable. Is it out of line to say that in a professional setting? Employees should be regarded based on their name.

25 Morgan Harwood, "Equal Pay for Asian American and Pacific Islander Women," *National Women's Law Center,* March 2019.

26 Ibid.

Audrey Gibson, a Florida Senator and African American, was called the "n word," "bitch," and "girl" by Frank Artiles, a Republican Senator.[27] He did not object the accusations, rather apologized and resigned after it was revealed he had directed the racial slur not only to Gibson but another black politician as well.[28] Gibson is a sixty-four-year-old woman who has been involved in government affairs for decades. To have your political career undermined and attacked—unprovoked—because of the color of your skin and your gender is appalling. As much as we'd like to convince ourselves people no longer behave and treat others like this, especially in a place of work, it is obviously far from the truth. No legal action, like having Artiles formally resign, will be able change the attitudes of those who deem treating women of color in a demeaning manner acceptable.

Today, we see many strong women of color in high positions who are incredibly young, and who worked hard to be where they are today—women like AOC, a United States representative who worked as a waitress for a few years before running for Congress, or Malala Yousafzai, a twenty-two-year-old Nobel Prize winner who was shot in the face for advocating for a girl's right to education. These powerful women broke the barrier for other women just like them, and are now the voice of a much larger group of people. This is just the start, though, and while we have a long way to come in achieving a sense of unison and a true feeling of the word "equal," every

---

27   Patricia Mazzei, "Miami State Senator Curses at Black Lawmaker—and Refers to Fellow Republicans as 'N****'." *Miami Herald,* April 18, 2017.

28   Ibid.

step in this movement is a step for every woman across the globe.

CHAPTER FOUR

THE US AND WAGE GAP

———

Women's concerns in the workplace are not limited to sexual harassment, unpaid maternity leave, and gender discrimination.

In the United States, women hold an average salary of $45,097 while men have a yearly average salary of $55,291. So essentially, women are paid eighty-two cents for every dollar that men earn.[29]

An abundance of factors contributing to the gap exists, and I honestly don't think I'll be covering half of them. I could throw a bunch of statistics at you, but those have already been overlooked and justified. Instead, I'm going to talk about the trajectory of a woman's career: why many women choose to leave their jobs, the astute hiring process that consequently works against women, and the complexities of a workplace environment.

———

29   "Women's Earnings: The Pay Gap," *Catalyst*, March 2, 2020.

Many women are forced to make a choice between having a career and starting a family. A choice no woman should still have to make in this day and age, and a choice most men rarely have to make. I watched my mother, a pediatrician who went to school for almost a decade, leave her work behind to take care of me after I was born. She began to work part-time as I got older, but those hours were nothing compared to the amount of time she spent taking care of me and cleaning up after my messes. Of course, having a child is a massive responsibility, but somehow, the one person who is always expected to make the most sacrifices is the mother. It is "her job" and "her duty" to leave everything she worked for to raise a child for eighteen years. Many mothers would willingly leave behind their careers to focus on starting a family, but you have to wonder if this choice is really a choice or the "only option."

It is not wrong to want to put a halt on your career and raise children, but there are a multitude of factors that make being a homemaker seem like the best option. Due to some patriarchal double standards that have yet to fade from society, women are generally expected to be the primary caretakers of their children (which many share the responsibilities with a husband). While battling this standard is a whole other issue, women are also at risk of losing their job if they decide to ask for a longer leave. There have been multiple cases about employers that give their female workers a hard time if they ask for an extended maternity leave and/or paid leave, and there has been even more speculations some companies and their employers hire less women for this very reason. While many companies have a human resource department specifically trained to identify and handle these gender biases, men in powerful positions are able to work the system right under their nose.

According to the law in the United States, women must be given up to twelve weeks in the case of pregnancy or childcare.[30] This does not mean women are paid during that period of time because paid leave is usually a case-by-case issue. In the working world, three months is a lot. In three months, a company could make major regression or profit, there could be a shift in the structural hierarchy, or a change in the mission or goals. Companies don't have time to hire women that decide to tend to their family's needs first, and therefore avoid seeking and hiring women altogether.

About twenty thousand women have made reports of sexual discrimination and sexual harassment in the workplace *every year,* and what's even scarier than this number is the amount of cases that are never reported.[31] Some women fear they will lose their job, other women are threatened into keeping their mouth shut, while many are bribed into remaining silent. Some women are even embarrassed, taking us back to the very nauseating victim blaming that some people use to justify assault. One of the biggest recent sexual harassment cases you might remember was the 2016 lawsuit against Roger Ailes, the ex-CEO of FOX News. Gretchen Carlson, a news reporter for the channel, made sexual harassment allegations against Ailes, claiming he failed to renew her contract after

---

30 "Family and Medical Leave (FMLA)," *U.S. Department of Labor,* accessed May 4, 2020.

31 Tara Golshan, "Study Finds 75 Percent of Workplace Harassment Victims Experienced Retaliation When They Spoke up," *Vox,* October 15, 2017.

she refused to sleep with him. He made similar incessant comments for the years they worked together.[32] Ultimately, after winning the lawsuit and receiving a smashingly heartfelt apology from FOX, she left the channel. Carlson is not the only woman to accuse Ailes of sexual harassment: twenty-three other women he worked with made similar allegations, all of which went unnoticed or dismissed.[33] Many of these women have gone on to write about their experience working with him in detail. Their encounters were ranging from unsolicited flirtatious advances to attempts at kissing them behind closed doors.

Women have a harder time fighting these advances and uncomfortable situations, especially in work forces where their boss is a man and the majority of the people they work for or with are men. It feels like if you "out" yourself, there won't be many people by your side for support. I feel like it is important for me to say that, of course, many male employees do not contribute to these uncomfortable scenarios, but when cases of harassment or assault arise, a female employee cannot expect support from her co-workers.

To paint another scenario into perspective, women are actually more likely to ask for a raise or promotion and not get one. However men are more likely to be given a raise when they ask for one.[34] Women are more prone to being verbally

32 Emily Crockett, "Here Are the Women Who Have Publicly Accused Roger Ailes of Sexual Harassment," *Vox,* August 15, 2016.

33 Ibid.

34 Janet Nguyen, "Men and Women Ask for Pay Raises at the Same Rate— But Men Get Them More Often," *Marketplace,* June 10, 2019.

degraded and scrutinized by their employers and co-workers for showing any semblance of pride, ambition, leadership, or confidence in their own capabilities.

An argument I consistently hear is women are generally attracted to the humanities, and therefore obtain degrees in fields that do not pay as well. The argument is because women tend to be more nurturing and in touch with their emotions, they tend to go for jobs that reflect these characteristics, which in turn, pay less. Why is it that people continually try to justify their misogynistic ideals by throwing around BS "facts"?

Men had a hard time sharing the same lab table with women for far too long, and for this reason, women were discouraged from joining the field of science and technology until the late 1990s, when it became more socially acceptable to do so. There were a few women that joined the field knowing the hostile environment they would be forced to work in. I remember learning about Rosalind Franklin in my high school biology class. My teacher refused to follow the school textbook that accredited James Watson and Francis Crick and their (version) of the theory on DNA because it simply was not their original work. Rosalind Franklin was a chemist who worked on the theory of DNA from 1938 until her death in 1950.[35] Her work was so utterly disregarded by other male scientists at the time that another scientist helped the two noble peace prize recipients steal and receive credit for her research. Her work was largely ignored in the field for

---

35 Beryl Lieff Benderly, "Rosalind Franklin and the Damage of Gender Harassment," *AAAS*, August 1, 2018.

decades, and though her name has a sort of familiar ring to it now, most people still identify the discovery of the DNA structures with the two male scientists. Franklin, a Jewish female and a double minority, was working in a predominantly male field. She often worked on her own. She worked in a separate laboratory from her male counterparts to avoid their blatantly sexist and degrading comments. Crick, one of the scientists who was accredited for her work, admitted he could be rather patronizing toward her.[36] Because anti-Semitism was running rampant during this time, she could not avoid racial discrimination from her colleagues, either. Her father warned her of the inevitable sexism and racism that was to take place in her workplace, but that did not stop Rosalind Franklin from dedicating her time to a field she was truly passionate about, all the way up until her death.

Many other women have similar stories to Franklin (Ever wonder why J.K. Rowling never used her real name when she published her books?) that fly under the radar because it has just been so easy to step all over women for so long. The reason we don't see as many women as men in non-humanities fields (though I'd like to point out the numbers are growing) is because it takes time for groups of people to bounce back from centuries of historical oppression. Think about any other group of people that was oppressed in the past and apply that same logic to this situation. Many African Americans and Latinos are born into impoverished families in cities and, unfortunately, not everyone can break free from the cycle of disparity that continually oppresses their people.

36 Beryl Lieff Benderly, "Rosalind Franklin and the Damage of Gender Harassment," *AAAS*, August 1, 2018.

It's the reason people seek help from the government and we have implemented certain policies that are designed to benefit a group of people (like affirmative action). Systemic inequality has made it difficult for people of color to close this wealth gap, regardless of education, age, gender, or income. An article from the Center of American Progress writes that the median income for a black family with a college degree is 70 percent of a white household *without* a college degree.[37] It's an appalling truth that we have yet to see make any sign of progression. So when I hear people complaining about how easy it is for women to get into certain fields simply because of the fact that they are female, I'd like to believe this person is uneducated in regards to the effects centuries of oppression can have on a group of people even in present day.

When I think of my friend and her father's unfounded assumption on her ability to do physics, I get so upset because this means women are discouraged from doing certain things from the time they are little girls. It becomes something that is engrained inside their minds, and something that will most likely follow them for the rest of their careers, as they subconsciously wonder whether or not they can even do something because of something they cannot change.

---

37 Angela Hanks, Danyelle Solomon, and Christian E. Weller, "Systematic Inequality," *Center for American Progress,* February 21, 2018.

CHAPTER FIVE

RACIAL STEREOTYPES PORTRAYED IN MEDIA

———

Hollywood is infamous for its underrepresentation and misrepresentation of minority groups in movies, television shows, and multiple variations of visual medias.

Racism and America have had an intricate and ruthless history that has extended to the twenty-first century; the post-racial social paradigm that has convoluted American thinking is the notion racism no longer exists. A pop-culture film that exemplifies this paradigm is the critically acclaimed film *Get Out*. Jordan Peele's film critiques systematic racism and racial liberalism, concepts that are rarely discussed and often overlooked yet still remain prevalent in present-day society. The film exposes the disregarded post-slavery era of institutionalized racism and racial liberalism.

The contemporary American claims how "woke" they are through the notion that they are simply blind to race. Let's look at an example of a modern film that perfectly exemplifies the microaggressions that still exist in our society: *Get Out*. I believe this movie is a perfect example of how covert racial stereotypes are still manifested in today's "liberal" societies. Jordan Peele portrays the common ignorance and the marginalization of African Americans through a complex plot and set of characters in this stimulating piece of art. While visiting his girlfriend's family for a weekend, Chris, a young African American man, comes to realize he is in the presence of white liberals with malevolent intentions. Through the hypnosis of Chris, Peele introduces the concept of a "sunken place," a dark hole most blacks are thrown into while being forced to inhabit the theory that their discomfort in the presence of whites has nothing to do with their race. Jordan Peele himself describes the sunken place as a symbol for marginalization. Regardless of how loud they scream, the system of oppression is even louder.[38]

The idea that Chris knew he had to get out before he even got in, yet remained in an uncomfortable atmosphere, attributes to the political agenda that equates racial blindness to the concept of wokeness. His fear from the beginning of his stay all the way to the end, is a result of the concept that blacks must remain quiet when dealing with an issue of race, as race is no longer an issue at all in a color-blind and liberal society. While almost all white Americans have black friends, relatives, co-workers, and acquaintances, and probably even would have voted for Obama for a third term if they could, they are contributing to the anti-blackness attitude and

---

38 Zack Sharf, "'Get Out': Jordan Peele Reveals the Real Meaning Behind the Sunken Place," *Indie Wire*, November 30, 2017.

arrogance that affects the common black woman or man when eluding their liberalism to the denouement of racism.

Get Out is an American horror story that has more truth to it than any film in its category. While it falls into the genre of fiction, the film's storyline and central theme are elements that are all too familiar to certain groups of minorities. It portrays the dismissive characteristic of white liberalism—an insidious set of beliefs that has taken over the contemporary American and their politics—leading them to believe they live in an era of post-racialism, a country free from prejudice and discrimination. While blacks no longer face *blatant* racism in the form of slavery and segregation, the attitudes and behaviors of white liberals will continue to formulate and shape the nation's backbone—one that builds on apparent racial injustices with inconspicuous ones.

***

Stereotypes and microaggressions are not limited to the black community. Asian Americans and Latinos have also had a long history of degradation in the hands of their oppressors, which is present today in the form of disparaging portrayals in media. While *Get Out* proved to be a paradox of the faultiness of white liberalism and microaggressions, Asian Americans and Latinos are still struggling to create films that do not fall prey to a false perception of their cultures.

Asian Americans in film and media are often misrepresented in the form of limiting roles that abide by the hegemonic status quo of Hollywood as well. The use of the Asian American as a scapegoat dates back to the early twentieth century.

Because Asian Americans tend to remain silent about their roles in television and film, Hollywood portrays the group in any way they choose.

Typically, we don't see a lot of South Asians in Hollywood, but when we do, they are often downplayed for their culture and background. The most predominant role for a South Asian actor or actress is the nerdy sidekick—the man or woman usually gets three lines in every episode and always seems to be overlooked by stronger characters. I know we're all thinking of Raj from the Big Bang Theory. He is unable to speak to women, has strict immigrant parents who want him to get an arranged marriage, and is the only main character on the show with an accent. Because Indians are rarely portrayed in film and television, the roles they play have a massive impact and leave a lasting impression on their audience.

Much of the misrepresentation of East Asians in Hollywood correlates with the Eurocentric image of Asian Americans, dating back to the age of colonialism. Colonialism emphasized the white man's duty to rescue the helpless, such as in the case of an Asian woman from the hands of the abusive Asian man. Since Hollywood's earliest days, Asian women have been represented as aesthetically pleasing, sexually willing, and/or dark and primitive. The two most pertinent roles in media today are the mysterious "Dragon Lady" and the docile "Madame Butterfly." The Dragon Lady is sexually and morally corrupt; she displays an attitude but later gives into her lust.[39] A modern example of the Dragon Lady is Nagini

---

39 Jacky Dang, "Asian Stereotype of Dragon Lady Rises in *Fantastic Beasts 2*," *AsAm News*, November 21, 2018.

from *Fantastic Beasts 2: The Crimes of Grindelwald.*[40] Nagini is a female character, played by a Korean actress, who transforms into a snake. Clad in dark clothing, while maintaining a mysterious persona and literally being imprisoned behind bars, Nagini proves Hollywood is persistent in its outdated portrayal of female Asian characters.

Madame Butterfly is not as outspoken as her counterpart. She is passive and subservient. Today, the Madame Butterfly has been slightly altered to look like the white protagonist's Asian sidekick. Seen in rom-coms and television shows (think Lane from *Gilmore Girls*), the Madame Butterfly is always timid and rarely takes the stand unless prompted to. Ultimately, both female roles play out perfectly for the male protagonist.[41]

These repetitive and misrepresentative roles have insidious effects on audiences as well. Studies show the constant images of these docile, oversexualized, or unethical women have a psychological imprint on audience members.[42] It isn't a coincidence pornography websites have an "Asian" category. It appeals to those that would like to view submissive and complacent women, similar to the role of the Madame Butterfly.

Currently, Asian Americans in Hollywood are working against the stereotyped and mythologized roles in visual media in creating portrayals of their people as one that is

40 Ibid.

41 Kent A. Ono & Vincent N. Pham, *Asian Americans and the Media:* Media and Minorities (Cambridge: Polity, 2009).

42 Ibid.

diverse and multidimensional. Asians have remained silent for decades about their false representation in film and television, but time has called for the destruction and reconstruction of the image of this minority group.

***

The Latino community happens to be the largest minority group in the United States, yet it is the most falsely depicted race in the media industry. The depictions of Latinos in visual media have predominantly been told by white writers, white producers, and white actors in "brownface," allowing for the false representation of Latino culture, background, and the emergence of outrageous stereotypes. The stereotypical roles in Hollywood are endless, but I have simplified the list down to three common characters: the promiscuous woman, the criminal, and the clown. The promiscuous Latina is overtly sexual and constantly seeking male attention and validation (specifically from the white male protagonist). She is emotionally manipulative yet physically incapable of looking after her own well-being. The criminal, a role usually given to a Latino, is a violent bandit with a heavy Spanish accent signaling a feeble intellect.[43] He is irrational and abusive toward his wife or girlfriend, and is usually taken down by the white man at the end of the film. The clown, who can be male or female, is simpleminded and airheaded; he or she serves as the comic relief in a consequential scene.

---

43 Tre'vell Anderson, "4 Latino Stereotypes in TV and Film That Need to Go," *Los Angeles Times,* April 27, 2017.

The Hollywood Latina is the symbol of the colonial relationship between Latin America and the US: the land and brown women have always been viewed as some*thing* to be conquered.[44] They represent the white man's conquest: something that can be easily conquered and colonized. Due to this limited perspective, Latinas are often designated the role of the sire, the vixen, and/or the woman that cannot be satisfied by a nonwhite male. She has an ethnic look that is white enough for a Hollywood film, and white enough to be a temporary love interest. She is the white man's muse, falling into the voyeuristic gaze of the heterosexual male. From the hyper-sexualized eye candy to the boisterous maid, Latinas are constantly portrayed as one-dimensional and stagnant characters. Their growth in films and television shows is hardly shown, and oftentimes, their entire identity revolves around their ethnic and racial background.

Take, for example, Sofia Vergara's role in *Modern Family*. She is portrayed as a sexual and feisty woman who often refers to her Colombian background whenever she incites fights with her husband. Speaking of her husband, Vergara's character, Gloria, is married to a white man three decades older than her. He is clearly well off and constantly providing for his wife, ensuring her role as a housewife. Rarely are Latina women portrayed as educated, accomplished, or dominant. Rarely do they end up with a Latino man that is not a bandit, a drug lord, or an abuser. This stereotype of the Hollywood Latina portrays all Latin women as nothing more than an object meant for the pleasure of man, belittling

44 Berg Charles Ramírez, *Latino Images in Film: Stereotypes, Subversion, Resistance* (Austin: University of Texas Press, 2002).

the accomplishments of real Latina women who have come a long way despite society's constraints on ethnic groups.

The problem that arises from these normalized and reoccurring stereotypes is these images have existed for so long and they start to become the norm. Being influenced by one's surrounding environment is in human nature, and unfortunately, not everyone can think for themselves. Our falsified image and treatment of this minority group stems from the ways they are portrayed in the films and television shows we watch, the news channels we choose to play, and the commercials and advertisements that pop up on our screens.

As people are becoming progressively aware of these inaccurate representations in Hollywood, there has been a new emergence of films challenging the stereotypes that have gone on for so long. Films have the ability to subvert the system by countering stereotypes, displaying Latinos in their true nature, and challenging the norm that has been accepted by Americans and the film industry for several decades.

What we watch, what we see, and what we hear are what shape our opinions, our views, and our perceptions on culture, race, and society. It may seem like such a trivial matter to discuss, but many of these things have been integrated into our society and our minds without pause for question. Minorities are misrepresented in all forms of media, making room for misconceptions that, unfortunately, mold a dangerous and menacing society toward these ethnic groups.

CHAPTER SIX

THE HISTORY AND IMPACT OF SLUT-SHAMING

———

It is really interesting to hear about people's reasoning for calling women names like slut, whore, and hoe (the list of words is endless). Many people do not see it as a form of shaming, and the defensive responses toward being called out on using those words are borderline comical.

"What else would you call her?" People ask. Or, one of the denser responses, "I would call a man that, too."

But those words were not created and intended to be used toward men, and they do not have the same connotation that they do when used to describe a woman.

The word slut, among the other dozens of similar misogynistic words, is used to make women feel ashamed for participating in the same sexual activities a man participates in.

While a woman is a slut for having multiple partners, a man is a stud for doing the same thing. While men find it easy to brag about their body count, women keep it a secret because of the social status they might receive. While men are told they are biologically inclined to be less selective, women are encouraged to be as selective as possible. These unfortunate realities are solely based on the fact society has found a way to mark a woman's virginity as a sacred and holy entity, and once it has been taken away, a woman's status falls to a soiled and untouchable object.

Traditional gender roles constructed a sexual code of conduct that created a strong distinction between the behaviors of men and women. Women and men were identified as biologically and inherently different, their conduct reflecting the same.

In most societies, a woman's talents were limited to homemaking and child bearing (for as long as her body permitted). It was pertinent for her to be seen as pure, innocent, and respectful, of her family, her husband, and God. The man of the house would earn money for his family, and ensure his masculinity was kept intact by making all financial decisions and disciplining his wife and children. Women had no control of their bodies, including when they did or did not want to engage in sexual intercourse with their husbands. It is important to note there was no concept of marital rape until the 1990s, and there was barely any legitimate legal process for victims of rape and assault. Socially speaking, women were clad in plain clothes to ensure they did not stand out, and they even wore heavy layered dresses until the 1900s that were designed in a way to restrict all movements.

It was improper for a woman to be calling too much attention to herself, and dressing and styling herself in ways that were generally out of the norm was like asking for society to label you as sexually promiscuous. These roles and rules evolved over every century, and as time went on, women received more liberties than in the years before. These changes expanded toward rights for women not only by law, but in regards to social norms as well. Women began to show more skin, they went out without their husband or male companion, they made money for themselves, and they made the decision in who they wanted to court and marry. While many fought against these changes, changes occurred nonetheless. Women have been fighting for a long time, and while it may not seem like they still are (in many fully developed and first-world countries), it is quite the silent war.

Slut-shaming is a concept we unfortunately cannot call "history." It was prevalent in the 1400s, with the rise of religion and colonialism, and it is still incredibly prevalent now. A woman was labeled a "whore" for having interest in a man that wasn't the one she was supposed to marry—the man her family had set her up with, despite her displeasure and dissonance. A woman was also considered a "whore" for showing the slightest bit of skin. A woman was socially exiled and characterized as a "whore" for having a child out of wedlock. Today, we have dozens of synonyms for the word "whore" that have the exact same meaning. We shame women for all of the same things and more.

Today, the judgment that is passed based on what a woman wears has the ability to define her character and personality. Today, women are labeled as sluts for not only being the adulterer but for being the mistress. The dozens of derogatory terms for the "other woman" ensure the cheating man receives no repercussions, seemingly identifying him as the victim. Today, women are shamed for being receptive to a man's advances, yet if they rejected him, they would be called a bitch or a cunt for having standards. It is almost as though no matter what a woman does or what role she plays in the situation, she is the immoral one.

These words represent a dangerous type of thinking that extends beyond blatant sexism and misogyny. Here is something to think about:

You call a woman a slut for wearing a really short skirt, so what exactly changes your mind when that same woman gets raped by a man at a party that night? You say victims are not the one to blame, but what do you believe goes through the mind of a rapist when he takes advantage of a woman while feeling no remorse during or after the act? He takes advantage of her because he does not respect her or the right to her own body. He thinks she is a slut and she is "asking for it" because of what she is wearing, placing her in the wrong. I'm not even reaching when I use this example because it comes straight from real rape cases in the twenty-first century.

Brock Turner was sentenced to six months in prison for raping an unconscious woman on a college campus.[45] The case was highly publicized due to the nature of the crime, the appalling sentence, and the words spoken by Turner and his

---

45   Kim Lacapria, "Brock Turner's Father: 'The Girl Got No Punishment for Being a Slut,'" *Snopes*, September 9, 2016.

family during the trial. Brock's father was recorded saying the victim should have been punished for being a "slut" and she had a career in porn waiting for her.[46]

Most people can agree rape is wrong and women should have the same basic human rights as men, but cannot comprehend how slut-shaming has anything to do with it. Calling a woman by a list of names for what she wears, how many partners she has, and how she chooses to present herself are all pit stops on a path leading to rape culture, victim-shaming, and internalized misogyny. It is hard to understand how slut-shaming can evolve into something so malevolent, but there is no other explanation for these societal beliefs we have all become so accustomed to.

The simple question is: Why is there the need for unsolicited judgment toward someone who is not harming you? It is a question that pertains to a lot of issues, not just a woman's sexuality and/or sexual liberation. It is a question we often forget to ask because we are so caught up in defending ourselves and our choices.

"Slut" is a word that normalizes incomprehensible acts of cruelty and disgust toward women, and we need to stop this trajectory of abuse by respecting women enough to not call them those names for choosing to do what they please with their own bodies

---

46   Ibid.

CHAPTER SEVEN

NO: THE MOST CONTROVERSIAL WORD IN THE DICTIONARY

———

I've talked about the dangerous outcomes of rejection before, and it's probably something that will come up in this book on multiple occasions, simply because I, as well as many other women in my life, have dealt with the situation firsthand.

This story, my story, will be told in its entirety, because I believe every detail of every story deserves to be told and heard.

When I was a sophomore, maybe fifteen years old, this boy I barely knew had a crush on me. When I say "barely knew," I mean he sat in the back of my Chemistry class and I probably passed a paper to him or said "excuse me" at some point in the school year. That was the extent of our verbal communication. This boy would text me every day on an app that almost everyone in school had so they could make mass group chats for every class and circulate homework and test answers. That app is what got me through high school. I responded to his texts almost every time, which were mostly questions about class or sometimes even answers to the homework I hadn't even asked for. It was obvious he was into me, and it was also borderline uncomfortable because he was too afraid to talk to me in class but would constantly message me throughout the day. By the end of my sophomore year, everyone knew he liked me and everyone also knew "we were texting." Well, shit, I wasn't into him and I was too naive and timid to understand I didn't have to keep entertaining his daily texts. So instead of being straightforward or even ignoring him, I made up some bullshit about having a boyfriend and he immediately stopped texting me.

My senior year rolled around and the same boy and his friend group consisting of maybe some ten or eleven dim-witted individuals similar to him began talking shit about me. I mean like nasty, horrific shit. It was clear my "secret" admirer did not handle rejection well and had convinced his friends I was not a good person. I remember not handling the situation well when I heard what was being said about me. My blood was boiling, and though I think deep down I was more upset than anything, my anger took control of my actions. Confronting one of the boys in the group got me nowhere, and if anything, it made things a lot worse.

While those boys never had the courage to say anything to my face, they had a blast making jokes behind my back. I learned the group of boys made rape jokes about me. The boy I had encountered previously said he wanted to rape me and get me pregnant.

I continued to learn that these boys made all kinds of crude remarks about me, calling me names, and making vile jokes that were one step down from rape. Week by week, I learned more things that were being said about myself. I was a cunt. I was a bitch. One of my friends told me they threw darts at my face at birthday parties (if this book ends up failing miserably, at least I know I would make a great party favor). They even said they wanted to fuck my dog.

I dreaded going to school that year. I had over twenty unexcused absences and would continue to make up excuses for not having to go to school. When those lies didn't work, I would leave my house at 7 a.m. and hide in a store parking lot until I was sure my parents had left for work, then return to my bed and lay there for the rest of the day. I was so depressed, and though I never thought about killing myself, I stopped looking both ways before crossing the street.

My friends had an idea of what was going on during this time. Not the depressed part, but the vulgar and disgusting jokes that were not so discretely being made behind my back. They would offer me their pity and tell me "those boys are assholes" and I didn't do anything wrong, but they also continued to be friends with the entire friend group and never said anything to their face.

I don't really blame them. High school is rough and there's this constant pressure to please and be loved by everyone. Clearly, I didn't get the protocol. For a long time, however, I was fucking pissed. I was so angry that I couldn't see that my friends weren't actually there for me. I was angry that

I never called them out on it, and I was even angrier that I didn't realize I deserved better.

Putting anger aside, high school became a distant memory after graduation and I moved on with my life. I made new friends in college, I distanced myself from people I felt no connection with, and I was incredibly happy. But those words that were spoken, the rape joke in particular, has left a stubborn stain in my memory that I still can't wipe away no matter how hard I try. I think about it every now and then, and my emotions waver between sadness and disgust. I'd be lying if I said I had forgotten or forgiven. What boils my blood is not the fact they constantly verbally harassed or threatened me, it's that someone was allowed to get away with making threats and jokes about rape when there are so many victims of the actual crime.

One in five women will be raped in the United States. Twenty-three percent of college undergraduate females and 15 percent of college males experience rape or sexual assault through some form of violence.[47] Two-thirds of college students experience sexual harassment. Eighty-one percent of women and 20 percent of men that are raped experience short or long-term effects like PTSD.[48] Rape is a traumatic experience that never really leaves you, regardless of the time past or the attempts to heal.

Today, when I look back at everything that happened in high school, I am filled with sorrow. Before, there used to be anger,

---

47 "Campus Sexual Violence: Statistics," *RAIIN,* accessed May 7, 2020.
48 Ibid.

and then there was a brief moment where I forgot about everything and moved on from all the toxicity, but those intense emotions have evolved into despondency. I am sad because that boy believed what he said was okay. His friends believed what he said was okay. My friends' passivity proved what he said was okay. It deeply disgusts me knowing victims of rape probably hear these jokes often and are forced to remember painful memories they hoped to forget.

Most importantly, it hurts to know that there are people who do not understand the culture of rape, and it does not entail just the act itself. Rape is an act enabled by the *feelings* of power and ownership—the rapist feels as though they own their victim, their emotions, and their actions. The anger someone feels when they are rejected are enough to fuel the act of rape.

It took me far too long to understand that connection between my failure to reciprocate a crush and the things that were said about me shortly after. Being seventeen and having to deal with the little nuances that naturally follow this vulnerable age and stage of life, this was (hands down) the most traumatizing thing to ever happen to me. I did not process what exactly was happening, why it was happening, and how it was continuously happening. I just wanted to hear my name called during graduation and walk away without having to look back ever again. After a year had passed and I had spent some time away from the toxic environment to process the events, I finally understood how the word "No" had such a strong hold over the boys that spent their free hours tarnishing my name. Rejection took a sharp dagger into a boy's inflated ego and made him lose all control over his emotions and actions.

The events that transpired from the word "No" in my experience were extreme and intense, but undoubtedly a common episode that often goes unnoticed. Many women have to deal with the whiplash of rejection. The rumors, insults, and lies that are made about them and their character are just terms they have come to accept. Thankfully, my situation was all verbal and never actually acted upon, but so many women are not as fortunate (sad that not being raped for rejecting someone is considered fortunate, isn't it?).

We hear so many stories on the news about a girl that was found raped by some random man after she rejected his advances, and instead of questioning this fucked up mentality, we continue to send our thoughts and prayers to a family that is beyond repairable. Just about two months ago, a college student was raped and murdered in a parking garage by a young man who was catcalling her on the streets. She rejected his catcalls, and while no one knows what exactly was said, we can assume he made remarks on her appearance and made some reference to her coming over. Her name was Ruth George, and she was nineteen years old. Ruth, like most young women that are victims of aggravated assault and murder, was expecting to go home that night after a long day of classes. She never thought her life would come to such an abrupt end because of an ignored catcall on a Saturday night. Ask any woman over the age of eighteen, and I can guarantee you she'll say she's been catcalled at least once. It happens to me every time I go into the city or walk the streets of my college campus in the downtown area after 7 p.m. It has happened to women clad in jeans and a sweatshirt and women dressed in a mini skirt and heels. It has become so normalized and accepted by all—women and men—that we don't even question the act. We are not able to see the fine line between the constant and shameless objectification of women, and the rape, assault, and murder that takes away so many of their lives every day.

There needs to be an end to the normalization of rape jokes and "locker room" talk that consists of degrading women for humor and pleasure. We need to stop being complacent with catcalls and inappropriate behavior that makes women feel uncomfortable leaving their own home after dusk. People should be confident enough to defend a woman who is being verbally threatened or physically assaulted without fearing judgment or backlash from people who lack morality. These are the small steps that must be taken by every individual to spark change in our society, and end the ignorance that subjects women to become victims of these subdued misogynistic values.

PART II

CHAPTER EIGHT

RAPE CULTURE AND INDIA

———

A recent rape case in the news sparked an international-wide conversation about rape culture and the way society handles these cases and their victims.

Dr. Priyanka Reddy, a veterinary doctor in Telangana, India, was leaving her dermatologist appointment at a local plaza. Ready to head home, she found that one of her tires had been punctured.[49] Four men approached her and offered to fix her tire for her. As she waited for the strangers to repair her bike, she kept her sister on the phone, giving her updates on the incident. Priyanka told her sister she was scared. What happened next isn't quite clear, but Priyanka's body was found the next day, brutally raped, murdered, and burned fifteen miles from where she was last seen.[50]

---

49 Roja Mayabrahma, "Dr. Priyanka Reddy Case: The Brutal Rape and Murder That Left Entire Nation in Shock," *The Hans India*, November 30, 2019.

50 Ibid.

Rape culture is the normalization of sexual assault toward women due to certain societal and cultural standards that consistently blame the victim.[51] Countries who host patriarchal societies such as, but not limited to, India, have displayed this notion time and time again. In such countries, a woman's identity is limited to a mother or a wife, not a human with a job and defining characteristics that mark her as an individual. So when a woman is raped, people's first reaction is to point fingers at the victim and question her morality and judgment. "What was she wearing?" and "Why was she out so late?" However, Priyanka Reddy was fully clothed and was planning to be back home by 9 p.m. She couldn't possibly be at fault, even according to vile and outrageous victim-shaming standards. When the victim "asking for it" isn't even a plausible explanation for what happened that night, then what is?

Many third-world countries like India have a corrupt legal system that fails to serve its people. Police in India are infamous for their misconduct and failure to follow "proper protocol," even though it is questionable as to whether any protocol for these kinds of situations exist. In regards to rape and assault cases, it has been proven time and time again that police have little training on how to handle such situations, and Priyanka's case was no exception to this unfortunate pattern.

News reports show Reddy's family did not get an immediate response from the police station when they filed the report. After they had finally gotten a hold of the police, officers

---

51   "Rape culture," *Marshall*, accessed May 7, 2020.

suggested she may have eloped with someone and had not informed anyone of her whereabouts.[52]

About two weeks after the discovery of Priyanka's body and the identification of the four men involved in her rape and murder, all four suspects were killed in a cross fire.[53] The suspects were taken to the area where Priyanka's dead body had been found, and they were asked to reenact what happened the night of the murder. Chaos infused when the four men tried to make a break for the officers' weapons instead, and police had no other choice but to shoot them down.[54] It seems like a bizarre and almost "too good to be true" occurrence, but that's a theory I'll save for another time. One way to look at this incident is in a light of optimism: justice was served, and the men got what they deserved. One could also argue the four suspects never got to go to trial, have their identities exposed, and receive a proper punishment through the court. Regardless of your perspective on their sudden deaths, a young woman's life was taken away from her, and her family and friends will have to suffer the aftermath of her death for the rest of their lives.

In many countries, victim-blaming is integrated into society not just by the common man, but professionals as well. Police officers may bring their own bias to the table, including views that are often considered misogynistic. There have

52   Siddhant Pandey, "Priyanka Reddy Murder Case: Four Accused Arrested by Hyderabad Police," *News Bytes*, November 20, 2019.

53   Agencies, "'Hyderabad Horror' Rape-Murder Suspects Shot Dead," *World Asia*, December 6, 2019.

54   Ibid.

been several cases where women go to report a rape and/or assault and are met with victim-blaming accusations. Police give victims a hard time for reporting a case "late" or accusing a person from a higher socially-economic status. They oftentimes try to convince the victim to settle or bargain the case and not take it to court to save the man's, as well as her family's, reputation. Many doctors will encourage the victim to allow a conduction of the hymen test to determine whether or not a rape actually occurred. For those of you hearing the term for the first time, the test "detects" whether or not a woman's hymen is intact. This test is having the potential to become a crucial piece of evidence in disproving a rape.[55]

The hymen can break from all kinds of activities, many of which can occur at a very young age. Activities include riding a bike, stretching, strenuous exercise, and masturbation. In some cases, women are born with perforated and/or deviated hymens that never break during sex or simply have no tell that it has been broken (there is no blood).[56] The point is, the hymen test is an incredibly sexist way of not determining if a woman is still a virgin, rather ensuring she feels completely violated and degraded by the end of it. But more importantly, the hymen test is yet another way to shame women for having consensual sex. It implies that if a woman has already engaged in intercourse, her rape accusation is not quite as valid anymore. The hymen test is the vilest and completely inaccurate determinant of rape, yet many doctors

---

55   Harmeet Kaur, "So-Called Virginity Tests Are Unreliable, Invasive and Sexist. And Yet They Persist," *CNN*, November 9, 2019.

56   Amy Marturana Winderl, "7 Things People Get Wrong About the Hymen," *Self*, October 26, 2016.

get away with performing it on victims who may not be as educated about the female body in general. Being aware of the misconceptions of the female body would make victims less susceptible to the intimation behind this unreliable test.

Imagine living in the kind of society where publicly accusing someone of rape is the equivalent of dragging your family name in the mud and being sexually active prior to an assault makes your accusation invalid. These women are living in their own personal hell.

Reddy's case sounds similar to several rape incidents in India, where the victim is cornered by multiple men and brutally murdered after endless hours of torture. Where the police fail to efficiently work to solve the case and help the mourning family in every way they can. These types of rape cases display a level of inhumanity that is almost unimaginable, one that seeks to humiliate, disfigure, and demoralize the human woman. It is a level of inhumanity that views women not as individuals with feelings, aspirations, and goals, but rather meaningless objects who serve only for the pleasure and *disposal* of men.

Priyanka Reddy's death made the people of India angry. Women and men gathered on the streets of Hyderabad, the city where Priyanka was murdered, and demanded justice from the police department. They held signs, in Hindi and English, which read: "Stop Rapes, We Want Justice" and "Violence against women is not my culture."[57] They wanted

---

57 Shreya Bhardwaj, "Protests in Telangana Over Priyanka Reddy Rape-Murder Case," *India Ahead*, December 1, 2019.

to see the perpetrators go through a proper trial and be handed the death sentence, demanding capital punishment for the cruel attack. Many protestors also expressed their anger toward the chief minister for failing to make a public address about Priyanka's murder and for not paying a visit to her mourning family.

Every once in a while, a rape case gets sensationalized on the news to the point where the people who were once unbothered by such tragedies are all of a sudden moved: they are enraged and disgusted, and maybe even sad. But these feelings quickly wash over as time goes on, and people begin to talk less and less about what happened to that girl that night by those men for God knows how long. We can't forget, no matter what the media lets you believe is more important or more current. No matter how upset hearing about it makes you. No matter how busy you are with your life and your issues. Hundreds of women like Priyanka Reddy are raped every day in India, and their stories disappear into thin air, along with their young lives and bright futures. It is our job to remember them and use their pain to ignite a passion that will allow us to help other women who could be next at any given time. We have a responsibility to be the voice for women who had theirs taken away from them in an evil and senseless act.

If someone is being constantly hit on or flirted with and it is clear no reciprocity exists, say something. Many times, the actions leading up to an assault or rape are conducted in public. The tireless flirting and the unsolicited gestures by strangers are often privy to bystanders. If someone looks uncomfortable, it's probably because they are. If someone decides to tell you about an assault or rape they were a victim to, do not force them to go to the police or immediately seek help from another source, rather, try your best to provide them some sort of comfort and ease. It is important to seek justice, of course, but when something this traumatic happens to someone, giving them the power to speak is the best choice. Survivors are susceptible to mental disorders including depression, PTSD, and anxiety after their attack. One-third of rape victims develop PTSD and one-fourth of these victims will attempt suicide.[58] They are 30 percent more likely to develop major depression than a nonvictim, and they are four times more likely to contemplate committing suicide.[59]

There are only so many battles we can fight on our own. If you are a victim of rape or assault, know it was never your fault, and there are always people who think about you and care about your well-being.

---

58   "The Mental Health Impact of Rape," *National Violence Against Women Prevention Research Center,* accessed May 7, 2020.

59   Ibid.

CHAPTER NINE

ACID ATTACKS

———

I remember hearing about Laxmi Agarwal when I was really young, maybe five or six years old. Her face was all over the news in India, and it even made some headlines on American channels. Laxmi was fifteen years old when a thirty-two-year-old man threw acid on her face and body near a bus stop in New Delhi, leaving her skin to burn and melt as she fell into a state of unconsciousness.

Laxmi was attacked in broad daylight by her stalker and two other accomplices who helped him carry out the atrocious act. Her stalker, Naeem Khan, had been trying to court Laxmi for months. Prior to the attack, Khan would send her multiple messages a day, calling her time and time again to try to get her to speak to him when she ignored him in person. His desperate calls evolved into stalking Laxmi wherever she went. Just before the attack, he professed his love to her over text. Khan even asked Laxmi to marry him. She rejected him. This rejection infuriated Khan to the point where he decided to throw a beer bottle filled with acid onto the young girl's face, hoping to scar her permanently—ensuring that, if he could not have her, no other man could.

Acid attacks are most common in South Asia and the Middle East, with Bangladesh and Pakistan having the highest reported acid attacks. This number has been incrementally increasing over the past couple of years. In these countries, 80 percent of the time, the victim is a female and the perpetrator is a male, generally a rejected suitor or a husband who was just asked to sign divorce papers.[60]

Laxmi had to undergo multiple surgeries over the course of seven years to save her eyesight and maintain some facial features, but her physical appearance was permanently altered. In an interview with *Times of India,* she says she recalls looking at herself in the mirror after the surgery and wanting to commit suicide.[61] She says that when she went home, people's immediate concern was whether or not she would be able to find a husband now that her face was disfigured. Laxmi even admitted that she was afraid to tell her parents about Khan's advances prior to the attack because she believed they would put a halt on her education and have her stay at home, rather than confronting her stalker.[62] Laxmi was a teenager rejecting the flirtatious attempts of a man twice her age and yet, society found a way of making her feel responsible for the attack. The general concern was not over her well-being, rather the family image. Laxmi's attacker, on the other hand,

---

60   Bipasha Baruah and Aisha Siddika, "Acid Attacks Are on the Rise and Toxic Masculinity Is the Cause," *The Conversation,* August 13, 2017.

61   Neha Chaudhary, "Acid Attack Survivor Laxmi Agarwal: 'After First Two Surgeries, I Thought I Would Look Prettier Than Before'," *Entertainment Times,* April 11, 2019.

62   Ibid.

was released from jail on bail, and was not convicted for his crimes until nearly five years later.

So many emotions go into writing and reading about stories like this. My initial reaction was shock, and then bewilderment. It shocked me that it was this easy for someone to attack another human being and hurt them in a way that is so beyond inhumane. Then I felt anger when I read about why the act was committed—all because of an attack on a fragile ego. This anger and bewilderment finally evolved into sadness. I felt so shaken because I can't even grasp the kind of toll this must have taken on the young girl's life. Her life, along with a superficial yet eminent part of her identity, is changed forever. People will look at her in ways that will make it even harder to move on, and she will never be able to go out and do things on her own without feeling like the whole world is staring. All because of the word "no."

Laxmi, however, did not let her attacker win. Today, Laxmi is a television host and a campaigner for rights of acid attack victims. She founded "Stop Sale Acid," a movement that is fighting the sale of acid to mass public without restrictions.[63] Books and movies are being made about Laxmi as she continues to use her growing platform to bring awareness to those who were affected by a mindless act. Laxmi even has a young daughter, Pihu, who is being raised to be just as strong

---

63 Shruti Kedia, "Laxmi Agarwal's Story and How This Acid Attack Survivor Has Not Just Inspired Deepika Padukone, But Millions of Other Indians," *SocialStory*, June 17, 2019.

as her mother.[64] While Laxmi has a reputable career and is using her influence for the better, all she ever wanted was the chance to live a normal childhood. In interviews, she talks about how she wanted to be a singer. She wanted to go on *Indian Idol* and become a star.

If you looked at pictures of Laxmi from when she was a teenager, you would be shocked and maybe even baffled by what you see. She looked like a baby. She looked so much younger than she actually was during the time of her attack: fifteen. Her delicate features, her pure smile, her bright eyes, and her youthful skin bring nostalgic flashbacks of middle school and the earlier days of high school, when you would play outside with your friends and stay after school for clubs and get yelled at by your parents for coming home later than you promised. Laxmi never got to fully experience those little moments. They were all cut short by a senseless act that permanently changed an innocent life.

The word "No" has ironically proven to be one of the most complex terms in the dictionary. It has been taken from its original definition and misconstrued into a phrase with free interpretation and little face value. This simple-looking word has brought cases to court, and on several occasions, has single-handedly determined the outcome of a case. This small word has so much power in controlling, not only human emotion, but action, as well. It's scary how, the word "No," if

---

64 Paromita Chakrabarti, "I Feared the Sight of Me Would Scare Her... All She Did Was Snuggle up, and Go to Sleep: Acid Attack Survivor Laxmi," *The Indian Express*, November 22, 2015.

not anticipated, can cause people to insinuate damage that is quite literally irrevocable.

Laxmi's story is one of thousands in just the past decade alone. Many acid attacks go unreported, for reasons similar to rape and assault cases, where the victim is either too scared to speak up and/or feels threatened from the public and police. Reprisal suppresses women into submission and ensures that they can never escape the society and its laws, which work against the liberty and empowerment of females. I think that, after reading about rape and acid attacks and the senseless murders of women and girls in these countries, the first step in improving the lives for women on a global scale is by necessitating a change in the legal structure; every society needs a justice system that actively works to promote the equality and protection of women from such cruel and degrading practices.

Of course, acid attacks are not the only medieval practices being performed in today's time. Child marriage is still prevalent in certain parts of the world and sexual assault and rape is being committed at alarming rates. While there is no way to infiltrate the twisted minds of those who partake in such vile acts, there are ways in which we can prevent women from being victims of these situations. Laxmi's attack was not her fault nor her family's, but the normalization of an older man courting a girl that has probably not yet reached puberty stems from the belief that a female's ultimate purpose is to become bound to the house and her husband. Education can be put on hold if they are married off to a working husband, and it is not necessary for a girl to strive to complete all levels of schooling. However, the advocacy of secondary and tertiary education can seriously alter all aspects of a young girl's life. Organizations like Commit2Change work toward providing orphan girls the tools to achieving a secondary education by providing them with school fees, supplies, and training programs, as well as better nutrition and reliable health care. The organization believes that helping girls achieve a complete education will result in a lower chance of child or teen marriage, a higher income, and a better society. If an increase of 1 percent of girls in India complete their secondary education, there can be upward of five billion dollars added to India's GDP.[65]

Commit2Change is obviously not the only organization that is working toward a better life for females across the country. With many other groups enacting similar agendas in motion, India can continue to see a decrease in the number of acid attacks, child marriages, and cases of rape and assault. By raising awareness to communities that may not have access to a higher level of education and simultaneously giving young girls the right to one, thousands of girls will be able to live their lives, uncompromised, and free.

65   "Our Impact," Commit2Change, accessed April 29, 2020.

CHAPTER TEN

CHILD MARRIAGE IN THE MIDDLE EAST

———

I was an inquisitive kid growing up, and I wasn't scared of reading really dark things, things that young children probably shouldn't be reading. I remember strolling the aisles in Barnes & Noble when I was maybe eleven years old when I noticed a book that caught my eye: *I Am Nujood, Age 10 and Divorced.* Most kids wouldn't be drawn to an autobiography when the entire goosebumps series is waiting for them two aisles down, but I guess I have always been a little feminist. The cover was simple yet daunting: it was a picture of a girl in her burqa, staring straight at the camera, looking into the eyes of whoever dared to pick up the book.

The title was pretty self-explanatory, but I flipped to the back cover anyway to get a little more insight on the book's content. The book was about a Yemeni girl named Nujood who was married off at the age of ten. Her husband was in his thirties, and him and his family were incredibly abusive toward the girl. Not having anyone to confide in but herself, she decided she could not stay married to the man and fought to seek a lawyer who could help her case. The book was very detailed and explicit, and I remember not understanding a lot of things as I continued to flip through the pages. Every so often I would look up from the book and ask my mom, "Is this really real? Like does this really happen?"

My mom wanted me to read and learn things for myself, even if the context was as morbid as Nujood's story. She would tell me these types of tragedies happen all the time in places outside of America and Europe, and she's seen it happen to many girls growing up in India. She told me she never witnessed it in her little town, but she always heard stories on the news or from other kids about young girls getting married off in their early years.

I reread the book multiple times, and each time the details became more and more clear to me. Girls were getting married as soon as they hit their double digits to a man three times their age. They never finished school and were raised to do household chores. They were usually sent off by their fathers who didn't see them as a gift but rather a burden. In exchange for lifting this burden from their shoulders, the girl's family would pay her husband a sum of money, also known as dowry. The girl would be abused and violated by her husband and his family until she became accustomed to their household rules. Not too long after marriage, she would be forced to reproduce multiple children. This story is not uncommon.

Every year, twelve million girls are married before they turn eighteen.[66] Though these numbers are slowly decreasing, there are about 650 million young girls who have already been forced into marriage. One of the most prevalent regions in which child marriage takes place is the Middle East and South Asia. In Pakistan, about 21 percent of girls are married before they have turned eighteen.[67] Even more so, the number of underage girls that consent to marriage is below 4 percent.[68]

Imagine what that means in regards to marital rape, lack of education, and domestic violence toward women. These children are denied the right to an education and are forced to comply to their husband, who could be as much as four times her age. Because they are viewed as property (remember most of these girls are given away with dowry), they have little to no control over their bodies and are subject to sexual abuse and forced reproduction. Any signs of resistance may lead to physical abuse and degradation; Nujood, who initially tried to fight off her husband's sexual advances, was emotionally and physically abused daily at the hands of her husband and her in-laws.

Obviously, child marriage extends to males as well. In Iran, the legal age of marriage is thirteen for girls and fifteen for boys. However, the government does little to interfere in families that wed their daughters and sons below this "legal

---

66 "About Child Marriages," Girls Not Brides, accessed April 29, 2020.

67 Naila Inaya, "Muslim Conservatives Defend Practice of Child Brides in Pakistan as 'Tenets of Islam'," *The Washington Times*, August 29, 2019.

68 Ibid.

age."[69] Even more frightening is the incredibly low age of sexual consent, which falls at nine for girls in Iran.[70] I think I am stating the obvious, but that is not sexual intercourse, it would be categorized as sexual abuse. Children that young are not able to consent for themselves.

Child marriage has multiple consequences. It results in the end of an education for the young child being married. When a girl is taken from her home and placed into an unknown stranger's kitchen, she is not given the option to return to school. Statistics show that only 65 percent of girls in Pakistan are enrolled in primary school (45 percent in the poorest households), and 71 percent of these girls never end up completing it.[71]

As one can assume, if no emphasis is put on the girl's education beyond the third grade, she most definitely is not out and about seeking a job to provide for herself. A child bride no longer "needs" a viable education or a job in the labor force because of her new roles of a housewife and a mother. As Nujood recalls in her autobiography, the day she got her period was the day her virginity was taken. She was ten years old. She was viewed as a woman, at the age of ten, and was ready to conceive children. To repeat a phrase I've had to use time and time again, a woman is viewed as a commodity at the disposal of men and, in many cases, a reproduction

---

69 "Iran—Child Marriage Around the World," Girls Not Brides, accessed April 29, 2020.

70 Ibid.

71 ABC News, "You're a Girl in Pakistan, What Are Your Chances of Going to School?" *ABC News,* October 7, 2013.

machine with the purpose of producing as many (male) off-spring as possible.

Many of these marriages are also done within the family as a means of resolving a dispute between two families. In multiple cases, young girls are married to their cousins and distant relatives. Incest is the result of almost a quarter of these marriages. Incest not only results in miscarriages and failed pregnancies, but the spread of diseases and genetic mutations to the offspring. Child marriages have multipronged consequences that tear down the very core of a woman in these societies.

A 2014 study on child marriage shows how many people living in poverty are unaware of the repercussions of child marriage while being the victim of one.[72] The study was conducted in the urban slums of Lahore, Pakistan, where most women were married before they turned eighteen and had a child in their teen years. Nineteen women were interviewed by NGO workers and all nineteen of these women were married between the ages of eleven and seventeen. The majority of them did not understand the effects childbirth could and can have on their health, and most of these young women stood by in their parents' decision to have them married at a young age.

---

72 Muazzam Nasrullah, Rubeena Zakar, Muhammad Zakria, Safdar Abbas, Rabia Safdar, Mahwish Shaukat and Alexander Kramer, "Knowledge and Attitude Towards Child Marriage Practice Among Women Married as Children," *BMC Public Health* 14, no. 1148 (November 2014): 2-7.

For these women, having an education and the right to make decisions for their well-being are seen as rarities and something they could only dream of. The culture and society they dwell in has shaped them to believe being married and having children at a young age, becoming a housewife and leaving school, and obeying their much older husbands is normal. What could they compare their lives to if all the women in their lives lived through the exact same thing?

The thing we are fighting here are the outdated values that define females not as humans, but objects that can be used in trade and to resolve disputes. The certain values disallow women to make decisions for themselves and their own bodies. The ones that view daughters not as something to be cherished but something that creates a burden. The ones that carve out a path for a woman that results in an abusive and unhealthy life until her last days on earth. We are fighting the corrupt legal system, which allows the marriage of young children. One that deems thirteen as the acceptable age for marriage and allows men to take advantage of little girls that are in their single digits.

It's hard to reach out to these girls and women due to the barriers between our countries, but there are so many things that can be done to bring women out of this horrific state. UNICEF and the Women's Funding Network are examples of organizations that seek to increase the child marriage age to eighteen in all countries in the Middle East and South Asia. Many organizations like CARE and World Vision work with families and their children in impoverished areas to educate them about the detriments of child marriage.[73]

The more educated young girls are, the more unlikely they are to get married and escape child marriage. While the number of child marriage cases are narrowing, a need for legal action in many of these countries in the Middle East exists. And until the law declares otherwise, many young children will continue to suffer the consequences of this egregious practice.

---

73   Carol Olson, "16 Organisations Working to Stop Child Marriage," *The Pixel Project's,* December 6, 2013.

CHAPTER ELEVEN

WHAT IT MEANS TO BE GAY AND MUSLIM

———

It wasn't long ago America's LGBTQ community won its long-lived battle for equality: the right to marriage. Even our democratic and liberal president Barack Obama had struggled with the concept of same-sex marriage for decades before passing the legislation in 2014, which finally allowed all Americans to love who they love under the legal system. So it is not and should not be too surprising over seventy states and thirty countries have made sexual intercourse and/ or marriage between people of the same sex illegal under the court of law. Of these jurisdictions, six countries—Iran, Saudi Arabia, Somalia, Sudan, Yemen, and Northern Nigeria—have imposed the death penalty on any form of same-sex activity.[74]

———

74 Map of Countries That Criminalise LGBT People," Human Dignity Trust, accessed April 30, 2020.

While many of these countries' citizens follow a variance of beliefs and forms of religion, a majority of their people practice Islam. Many of the morals and values pertaining to these societies are constructed around the majority faith. In countries like Lebanon, Saudi Arabia, and Pakistan, Sunnis are the majority sect of the religion and follow a distinct and strict religious code, known as Sharia. Sharia is an Islamic "legal code," which prohibits the consumption of alcohol, drugs, partying, and premarital sex. The law also restricts sexual conduct between those of the same sex.[75] While interpretations of Sharia vary from one jurisdiction to the other, disobeying certain aspects of the code may call for extreme punishment.

Surveys and statistics have found Muslims' views on homosexuality are rather divided, yet law dictates the collective attitudes Muslims *should have* toward homosexuals. Some Muslims observe the belief Islam condemns homosexuality, therefore viewing it as an irreconcilable sin. While many stand by a different interpretation of the Qur'an, which urges everyone to treat each other equally. However, some insist homosexuality is an illness that requires "urgent treatment," or some kind of cure. Treatments include marrying the "diseased" off to a person of the opposite sex or prescribing the "ill patient" medicines and therapies designed to reverse their sexual orientation.[76]

Before I continue this chapter, I would like to emphasize that these views are not limited to any one faith or culture;

---

75   David Emery, "What Is Sharia Law?" *Snopes*, June 19, 2017.

76   Zvi Bar'el, "It's Not Easy to Be a Muslim Lesbian," *Haaretz*, June 24, 2018.

conversion therapy has been observed in Europe and the United States as well. However, while many people across the world still confide in this practice, there are no laws banning reparative therapy in Middle Eastern and African countries.

A little over a year ago, a Kuwaiti scholar went on live television to say that she found a cure for homosexuality, a "prophetic medicine," she claimed.[77] She believed that intercourse between two men is a sexual urge provoked by "science," and it *continues* to persist because of an anal worm that crawled into the man's body and is feeding on his semen. The so-called scholar said eating bitter foods would increase masculinity and kill the worm, in turn curing those sexual urges.

While you may think this is an obvious fabrication of science and a true exemplar of homophobia, many traditionalists conform to these affirmations. The scholar's statements not only feed the belief that homosexuality is a disease, *but* they also give hope to people by providing a "remedy" for the illness. It is important to note in Kuwait, homosexuality is a crime and the list of punishments for this debauchery is endless. Therefore, making these kinds of claims on Kuwaiti live television, while offensive and controversial to some, would not be met with much censorship and/or resistance.

Due to these prehistoric beliefs and superstitions, citizens who identify as LGBTQ+ are forced to conceal their sexual orientation and live lives that are not true to themselves. They go on to do what is expected of them, which generally

---

77   Mariam Nabbout, "Kuwaiti Academic 'Found Cure for Homosexuality.' But it's Not a Disease.," *Step Feed*, April 26, 2019.

consists of marriage and procreation. Many Middle Eastern and Asian countries, attributable to their patriarchal nature, are constructed around societies who promote homosocial behaviors. Holding hands in public, sitting close to each other in public places, and frequently hugging and kissing each other on the cheek is common between men. What does this have to do with being patriarchal, you ask?

Societies and cultures dominated by men promote traditional gender roles, discourage premarital sexual relations between men and women, and emphasize the segregation of genders. Certain public areas are gender specified and walking in public with someone of the opposite sex is looked down on (unless they are a relative). With young male teenagers and young adults spending most of their time together, many forms of physical contact are seen as innocent and considered the "norm." Americans would find themselves screaming "no homo" after lightly brushing hands with another man, while Middle Eastern boys would gladly and willingly hold each other's hands while making their way to school.

With these social interactions deeply integrated into society for multiple centuries, no overt "tell" gives a man's sexuality away, which makes it easier, in a way, for men to conceal their identities. In some Middle Eastern countries, like Saudi Arabia, for example, meeting spots for gay men have been identified and become known through word of mouth.[78] After the sun sets and the dark calls for silence, parking lots and alley ways become social arenas for men to meet and be true to their sexualities.

---

78   Nadya Labi, "The Kingdom in the Closet," *The Atlantic*, May 2007.

Unfortunately, lesbian women have a much more difficult time navigating around societal norms. It is nearly impossible for women in countries with stricter codes to leave their house without a male companion. Saudi Arabia's Sharia, for example, has made it punishable for women to be unchaperoned in public. With these stringent laws and extreme reinforcements, Muslim lesbians are rarely able to explore and understand their sexualities, which explains the low statistical numbers of Muslim women who identify as LGBTQ.[79] That being said, it is not impossible for Muslim women or men to come out, rather that it is incredibly difficult due to the fear of rejection from society and their families. Many lesbian and bisexual women describe their inner conflictions when coming to terms with their sexualities. Women who believe the Qur'an condemns homosexuality describe their struggle with God and their duty to be a good Muslim; other women reject their sexuality out of fear for their image in the eyes of society and their family.[80]

Families fear shame and dishonor. What society views of them and their family name is consequential; it is more important than the sexuality identity of their sons and daughters. For this reason, among a few others, honor killings are quite prevalent in these societies. Its victims usually being women and homosexuals.

***

79 Daniel Burke, "In a Survey of American Muslims, 0% Identified as Lesbian or Gay. Here's the Story Behind That Statistic." *CNN*, 2019.

80 Ilaria Bilancetti, "The Hidden Existence of Female Homosexuality in Islam," *Jura Gentium*, 2011.

Ahmet Yildiz was a twenty-six-year-old university student from Turkey who lived with his boyfriend in Istanbul. He kept his living situation a secret from his family, well aware of their homophobic stance antiquated with their strict religious and traditional beliefs, until he decided to come out to his parents a few years later. Ahmet's father insisted that he return to their home and seek "treatment" for his "illness," but he refused.[81] Shortly after building the courage to come out to his parents, Ahmet began to receive death threats from them.

Ahmet repeatedly went to the Turkish police and lodged complaints against his family, begging the district attorney's office to look into his case and possibly provide him with some protection. The prosecutor's office refused to initiate an investigation, and a few months later, Ahmet was shot dead by his father as he stepped out of his car to get some ice cream. The murder took place in 2008, and Ahmet's father is still currently on the run. While it wouldn't be hard to track down his father, as it is believed he is still in contact with his family, the court refuses to have another hearing, and so justice for Ahmet was never achieved. However, Ahmet's murder was labeled as the first honor killing in Turkey, and it sparked a massive debate on LGBTQ rights in Turkey and other Middle Eastern countries.[82]

---

81 Dan Bilefsky, "Soul-Searching in Turkey After a Gay Man Is Killed," *The New York Times,* November 25, 2009.

82 Nicholas Birch, "Was Ahmet Yildiz the Victim of Turkey's First Gay Honour Killing?" *Independent.*

The Turkish justice system failed Ahmet. Everyone who was aware of Ahmet's situation before his death was able to escape the consequences for their lack of action and apathy. Ahmet's case was never looked into properly—before or after his murder—mainly because of Turkey's conservative outlook on homosexuality and the LGBTQ community. While the laws are constructed to provide protection against all hate crimes (including same-sex activities and gender identity), the masses generally disapprove of homosexuality, and same-sex couples often face discrimination and harassment. The law itself does little to protect these groups of people when the people whose job it is to enforce it fail to recognize and adhere to it.

Obviously, it is hard to push an LGBTQ agenda onto a society that still deals with issues like child marriage, permitted marital rape, and gender bias in all areas of legal structures within the government. These social constructs are all in part due to traditional and extremist values, which are strictly enforced in many Middle Eastern and African countries. Moral code *is not* the only aspect of these countries that is influenced by Islam, and being that the very laws and regulations branching from their government are based off of sacred religious texts, opposing certain values is out of the question.

However, the criminalization of homosexuality and gender transitions is not entirely in part due to the religion's extremist adaptations. Of course, the foundation of such beliefs stem from some adaptation of the religion, but the education on homosexuality, or lack thereof, directly correlates with the continuation of such traditions and old-fashioned mentalities. In these societies, many people are not educated on the LGBTQ community and therefore, resist the notion of legalizing or changing the ancient laws that dictate sexual intercourse and marriage between consenting adults. Many adults in these countries lack an education altogether, and a direct correlation exists between that and this type of resistant and traditional thinking.

CHAPTER TWELVE

THE UNWANTED BABY

I remember moving into my freshman dorm and scanning the doors that surrounded mine, reading the names of the girls I'd be sharing the daunting communal bathroom with for the next two semesters. I'm not going to lie, half of the names were Asian and I wasn't even surprised, but I saw the name "Stacy" and thought, "Well at least there's a little diversity on this floor." Turns out Stacy was Chinese; she was born in America but attended middle school in China, before resettling in the states with her family.

She and I got close over our freshman year, and she became one of my best friends by the end of it. I got to know all about her old high school drama, her love for designer brands, and how determined she is to make a career for herself. I also quickly realized Stacy is probably the most independent person I know however, not necessarily by choice.

Her parents traveled back and forth between China and the US for work, and during this time she looked after her brother and sister while living with some relatives. Eventually, Stacy graduated high school and her parents relocated to California with her siblings, while she stayed in New Jersey for college. I've learned a lot about her heritage and culture, and how her dynamic childhood shaped her Chinese-American identity.

Every now and then, Stacy will make passing remarks on American culture compared to Chinese culture, and how things are so drastically different between the two. Upon returning from China in her early teens, Stacy noticed a shift in family dynamic and structure, including the relationships between child and parent, husband and wife, and the young and the elderly. The hierarchy of a family and the expectations from each relationship are so profoundly distinct between the two cultures. She tells me she can't believe children talk back to their parents here, and shudders thinking about what her parents would do in their place. Stacy also talks about how women in America have so many more liberties—the freedom defined by culture. Even though she misses her family and her few years in China, she tells me she's happy to be here.

Sometimes, Stacy delves into her cultural findings without being prompted, and other times I ask her genuine questions which turn into hour-long discussions. I remembered us briefly talking about our family dynamics, and I'd ask her to tell me more about her traditional culture.

Chinese culture places a large emphasis on family values, including family structure, customs, and gender roles. Like many other East and South Asian cultures, being born female into a *traditional* Chinese family with stringent values has its immediate drawbacks and restraints. She shakes her head and rolls her eyes while she explains that female babies are never exactly preferred in a traditional Asian household. Oftentimes, couples will keep trying for a child until they conceive a son. Stacy isn't just reading from a textbook when talking about this practice. She has experienced it firsthand. She talks about how her relatives would always wish that the next baby born into the family would be a son. She scowls while telling me her younger brother, despite being the middle child, constantly gets more attention than her or her little sister. Her brother is often faced with more expectations in regards to education and careers as well. Meanwhile, Stacy's grandparents and parents bring up the discussion of marriage with her. They tell her she's already halfway into getting her degree, and it would take some time in finalizing a partner. She is twenty.

***

Female infanticide has existed in China for a long time, even before the One Child Per Family Policy was implemented in 1979. The practice of throwing newborns into lakes and rivers began in China in the sixteenth century, with the arrival of Christian missionaries. Previous to their infiltration, the act was severely condemned. In fact, it was believed that killing a female child would result in a fate met with pure evil. However, with the massive influence missionaries had over people at the time, the murder of female babies was regularly committed, particularly by those who could not afford a child. They were drowned, suffocated, and starved. They were placed in baskets, which were carefully hung from a tree branch, a practice later coined the "baby towers," and left there to die. People would walk past the baby hanging from a tree and mercilessly ignore its cries for attention. It is estimated that one-fourth of all female babies were murdered upon birth in the eighteenth and nineteenth centuries with one of these brutal methods.

Studies show that the policy added to the distinct gender ratio, and had an even larger effect on the boys who were being born into this city. Over the course of the policy's implementation, the crime rate in the country increased by 34 percent.[83] According to researchers and behavior analysts, growing up in an environment with much fewer women than men had an effect on males from the time they were children to their adult life.[84] The distinct gender disproportion lead to neurotic tendencies in many (of course not all) boys. Unstable behaviors lead to higher risk-taking behaviors and in turn, crime-related activities. While there are a variety of reasons given for preferring a son over a daughter, it is commonly believed sons are a vital element in providing for their parents as they get older. These traditional customs clearly place the female child as a burden, but they also create a burden for the son. He will continue to be expected to provide for his parents not only emotionally and physically, but monetarily, as well. While a daughter will be sent to her husband's house after marriage to take care of him and his family, a son and his new family will stay with his parents throughout their old age, tending to their needs. While a daughter will take on a new surname leaving behind her family name, a son will continue to reproduce and keep the family name alive.

---

83 Lisa Cameron, "China's One-Child Policy: Effects on the Sex Ratio and Crime," *Institute for Family Studies*, December 19, 2019.

84 Ibid.

If people were forced to maintain a family of three in China, wouldn't they rather have a son than a daughter?

Female infanticide is prevalent in many third-world countries. It is estimated , in the past twenty years alone, more than ten million baby girls have been aborted in India, meaning there is one female for every 1.7 males.[85] Pakistan and Middle Eastern countries show similar numbers. A horrific investigation from 2018 provided more evidence for the continuing practice, with 350 female babies found dead in Pakistan's capital.[86] These numbers are increasing in Pakistan and many countries in the Middle East, and while many Indian cities have made it illegal to disclose the sex of the baby upon sonogram, people have found loopholes around the law.

Steps have been taken to prevent such female infanticide, such as the Women's Protection Law in China, which prohibits infanticide and bans discrimination against women who choose to keep their female babies. In India, the Invisible Girl Project has a mission of rescuing unwanted baby girls who were abandoned on the streets, simultaneously preventing them from sex trafficking and abuse.[87] The Pixel Project is a global organization that raises awareness for domestic violence including sex-selective abortions through campaigns,

85 Sarah Boseley, "10 Million Girl Fetuses Aborted in India," *The Guardian*, January 8, 2006.

86 Julian Robinson, "Hundreds of Dead Newborn Girls Have Been Found Dumped in Garbage Piles in Pakistan Over the Last Year as Cultural Preference for Boys Drives More Parents to Murder Babies," *Daily Mail*, May 1, 2018.

87 "What We Do," *Invisible Girl Project*, accessed May 1, 2020.

donations, and funding projects.[88] However, no law that bans integrated sexism is enforced through patriarchal traditions, and there is no way to prevent families from treating their daughters, wives, sisters, and mothers like second-class citizens. These "traditions" continue to live on in Asian and Middle Eastern countries *and* families, and will unfortunately take decades upon decades to fully disintegrate.

---

88 "Violence Against Women," *The Pixel Project,* accessed May 1, 2020.

PART III

CHAPTER THIRTEEN

YOUNG GIRLS IN SOUTH AFRICA

———

Just about two decades ago, South Africa broke away from the apartheid regime and built their own democracy. One of the biggest challenges in doing so was establishing social values and principles that would give every citizen the ability to grow and exercise their freedom in an equal manner, regardless of their gender or social status.

The apartheid remained unscathed from 1940 to 1994.[89] Race was defined by the Population Registration Act of 1950 that classified all South Africans as white, native (black), or colored (those who were neither black nor white).[90] During this time, these three racial groups were developed separately within the borders of the country; this meant individual

---

89 "Apartheid in South Africa: Laws, End & Facts," *History*, accessed May 1, 2020.

90 Angela Thompsell, "Racial Classification Under Apartheid," *ThoughtCo.*, September 1, 2018.

races were raised, educated, and forced to live in different communities. Interracial marriage was banned, the socialization between different races was forbidden, and permission to enter certain public places was indicated by color of skin.[91]

This was obviously a horrific system that led to the inequality of races, not just socially, but economically and politically as well. While the majority of the population received a limited education (if they received one at all), men—particularly white men—remained at a clear advantage over the country's women, with access to higher learning resources and educational experiences. Women were also discouraged from joining political forces and voicing their opinion regarding laws and regulations, and were often only granted ownership and property rights if they were the daughter or wife of a property-holding male. Black women were prompted to stay at home and raise children, and were often subject to domestic violence, sexual abuse, and sexually transmitted diseases. Over the course of the apartheid, however, women were able to establish their own political organization, Alexandra Women's Council.[92] While the AWC made large steps to lower crime rates against women and the black community, members of the council faced constant risk of assassination and/or imprisonment. The majority of South African women and girls were and still remain a triple marginalized group in the sense that they are female, black, and socioeconomically disadvantaged.

91 "Apartheid in South Africa: Laws, End & Facts," *History*, accessed on May 1, 2020.

92 "History of Women's Struggle in South Africa," *South African History Online*, accessed May 25, 2020.

The country has a very complex history that has left a mark on their society, and the lingering effects have taken a toll on young girl's lives from the day they are born in South Africa. South Africans largely followed some form of traditional tribal practice until colonizers invaded their land in the seventeenth century.[93] Protestant practices spread across the country by British ministers and Calvinistic beliefs brought by French settlers merged to birth the Afrikaner religious doctrine. Afrikaner religious beliefs have a strong emphasis on the notion that women's contributions and activities in society should normally be approved by or done on behalf of men.

South Africa's society is structured upon incredibly patriarchal values. One of the most traditional beliefs is girls should focus on their roles as home keepers and child bearers from a young age. For this given reason and other "familial commitments," many girls do not have an education beyond the secondary level. Due to the rampant spread of sexually transmitted diseases in impoverished areas within the country, oftentimes daughters are forced to look after their sick family members and have no choice but to drop out of school. Girls are victims of sexual assault and harassment at school, with teachers, as well as classmates, holding the role of the abuser. From the time they step out of the house until the minute they return, girls are at risk of being kidnapped, raped, or murdered.[94]

---

93   "Afrikaner," South African History Online, accessed May 1, 2020.

94   Girls and Women," Africa Educational Trust, accessed May 1, 2020.

With a hostile environment and/or no family support, girls are discouraged from attending school and are choosing to remain at home even when they have access to some form of education. Imagine being too afraid to go to school because you fear your classmates will hurt you, and your teachers will not do anything to stop it. Imagine confiding in a teacher, principal, or authoritative figure, and in return, they use your trust as a way to commit a heinous crime. Girls find it easier to leave school behind and pursue a career as a mother, housewife, or work in the fields because those are the only roles they believe ensure their safety.

Colonization also introduced customs that were new to the country. Many South Africans believe that having sex with a virgin rids a man of HIV/AIDS, a sick myth that is still practiced to this day. While the origins of virgin cleaning are unknown, it has been speculated that the practice emerged from sixteenth century Europe. Virgin-cleansing contributes to infant rape, and it has also led to the spread of sexually transmitted diseases in very young girls. Unfortunately, about 20 percent of the labor population believes in this myth.[95]

South Africa reportedly has one of the highest numbers in sexual-violence related crimes. One in four men in South Africa admit to rape, many also confessing they have raped

---

95 Suzanne Leclerc-Madlala, "On the Virgin Cleansing Myth: Gendered Bodies, AIDS and Ethnomedicine," *African Journal of AIDS Research* 1, no. 2 (June 2018): 87-95.

more than one woman.[96] What's even scarier is only one in nine rapes are reported, meaning the men who commit such acts are most likely continuing to commit the act. This again brings up the issue of education, or the lack thereof. Many men who commit these heinous acts genuinely believe what they are doing is not wrong.

Much of the working and labor class have little to no education, and oftentimes it happens to be that none of the members of a family ever even went to school. Due to the aftermath of the apartheid and residual effects, many black communities do not have access to resources that allow for education beyond the primary level. Young children, especially girls, work alongside their mothers and fathers, working in the fields and around their home. While the actions are not justified and all victims of rape deserve their justice, it is clear educating both women and men will be extremely beneficial for the betterment of their society as a whole.

***

In 2008, Eudy Simelane, a thirty-one-year-old South African football player, was gang raped and murdered in her own hometown.[97] Once the motive for her murder became clear, all shock dissipated. Eudy was one of the first well-known South African woman to come out as a lesbian. She was regarded as a living icon, and many young girls and women looked up to her for her ability to defy the traditional gender

---

96 "Rape Statistics by Country 2020," World Population Review, accessed May 1, 2020.

97 "Eudy Simelane," South African History Online, accessed May 1, 2020.

female role. While her legacy lives on today, Eudy's death became an example of corrective rape. Corrective rape, or the rape of lesbian women in the hopes of turning them straight, is a horrific practice that is committed thousands of times a year. It generates the belief women should maintain their femininities through heterosexuality, but it also maintains the power men should have over women. The belief that rape demonstrates masculinity drives many young men involved in gangs to commit the act to "prove themselves." Eudy's rape murder, like many corrective rapes, involved four perpetrators. It is not a reach to conclude many of these men are pressured and encouraged to take part in these rapes to maintain a sense of masculinity imposed by society.

These tragedies hardly cast a shadow on the lives of people who are fortunate enough to be able to continue to go to school or work and have the resources to work toward their goals. But thankfully, mass organizations like UNESCO and UNICEF are working toward providing an all gender inclusive education for children around the world. UNESCO has a goal for their 2030 agenda which aims to "ensure inclusive and equitable quality education and promote lifelong learning opportunities for all."[98] The organization plans on working with state, local, and country governments as well as other local agencies in the hopes of achieving this massive goal. UNICEF has also worked to implement Girl Education Movement (GEM). GEM is a child-led grassroots movement where children still attending school and communities throughout Africa work to make a more comfortable learning environment for African students, both male and

98 "Leading SDG 4 - Education 2030," UNESCO, accessed May 1, 2020.

female.[99] Girl Education Movement aims to give girls easier and equal access to education, improve the quality of education especially in rural areas, create a school curriculum that is gender inclusive (for example, reproductive health and sex education), create an environment where girls feel safe and welcomed, and decrease child marriages.

Young education unionists are also working within the country to provide education for all, regardless of gender or class. Organizations like Southern Africa Women in Education Network (SAWEN) have raised awareness on gender disparity and have encouraged women in villages and impoverished states to join the cause and become members.[100] They invite women from all different African countries and hold a meeting in South Africa to discuss the ways in which they can work to achieve the United Nation's goals in regards to female empowerment and education. In their more recent agenda, they are working toward increasing the participation of girls in school and school-related events, creating a stronger teacher union to educate more females, and fighting against gender-based violence in schools.

These organizations are working hard to achieve their mission, and it shows. Statistics prove there is an increase in the number of young girls receiving an education. A recent study shows elementary schools have roughly the same enrollment

99 "10 Facts About Girls' Education in South Africa," The Borgen Project, accessed May 1, 2020.

100 "Southern Africa: Young Female Education Unionists Will Strive for Quality Education for All," Education International, accessed May 1, 2020.

numbers for both girls and boys.[101] If we continue to show our support for organizations with effective "call-to-action" and raise awareness about disparities, we have the ability to broaden the horizons for generations of South African children.

101 "10 Facts About Girls' Education in South Africa," The Borgen Project, accessed May 25, 2020.

CHAPTER FOURTEEN

SEX WORK IN RUSSIA

A common misconception is prostitution in Eastern European countries has become glamorized due to the increasing number of sex workers over the past decade. What many people fail to understand is prostitution in these countries is just as illegal as it is in the majority of other countries, and the sole purpose of sex work is the financial benefits that come alongside it.

A notable rise in prostitution in Russia can be seen in the late nineteenth and early twentieth century: the economy was failing, jobs were limited, and lower class women were desperately seeking jobs to support their families.[102] Many women began to leave their homes in the village and suburban areas and look for jobs in the city, where there were more opportunities to make a living.

---

102 Barbara Alpern Engel, "St. Petersburg Prostitutes in the Late Nineteenth Century: A Personal and Social Profile," *The Russian Review*, 48, no. 1 (1989): 21-44.

However, patriarchal standards were (and still are) deeply embedded into society, and that made it especially difficult for a single and independent woman to find a decent job in the city alongside other men. Oftentimes, receiving a job with a livable wage results in transactional sex: young girls are promised a minimum wage job in exchange for sex. Desperate and in need of a stable income, many of them give into the offer. Once these young girls realize that transactional sex is a well-established concept in the city, which in turn branches into prostitution, they give up their low salary jobs to become full-time sex workers.

According to a European news article from 2017, the average Russian citizen's income is on a steady decline by about 3 percent.[103] Most citizens do not have any savings, and more than one-third of the population is in severe debt.[104] This is largely due to their corrupt government and the failing economy. Most families survive off of loans and credit cards with heavy interest rates, which only keeps adding to their debt. The same article highlights the increase in air and water pollution; Russia's air quality is now a health hazard to civilians. The mortality rate increased by nearly 400 percent. Financial struggles have a toll on mental and physical health, as well as relationships with loved ones. A recent study concluded more than 60 percent of new marriages end up in divorce.[105]

---

103 Paul A. Globe, "'Russia Now Has More Prostitutes Than Doctors, Farmers, and Firemen Combined' and Other Neglected Russian Stories," *Euromaidan Press*, August 20, 2017.

104 Ibid.

105 Elena, "Divorce Statistics in Russia," *Elena's Models*, November 29, 2018.

Russian women are particularly struggling, with an average monthly income of twenty-eight thousand rubles, or about $423 USD, a barely livable wage.[106] They make 26 percent less than their male counterparts, and while this number is continually narrowing, it puts women at a major disadvantage that, in turn, leads them to take desperate measures: prostitution and escorting.[107] Because women are also largely underrepresented in the political structure, holding about 15 percent of seats in parliament,[108] little is being done to close the gender pay gap and decrease the rise of sex work. The sad reality is prostitution will continue to increase until women are given the same opportunities to obtain a livable wage.

Prostitution is the absolute last resort for these women, and arguably the most dangerous method to make some money. No woman chooses a life of prostitution with pride or assurance, but many believe it is their only option to support themselves and their families. Most prostitutes are in fact mothers—90 percent of them to be exact[109]—and they put their lives at risk every day when they step into a stranger's car or a dingy motel room for a couple bucks. Moreover, prostitutes do not get to pocket all of their earnings; if they work for a salon or a pimp, they end up forking over half of their income. Many prostitutes choose to operate out of a

106 "Women in Russia Earn Significantly Less Than Their Male Counterparts," *The Moscow Times*, September 15, 2017.

107 Ibid.

108 "30% of Russians Are Against Women Participating in Politics," *The Moscow Times*, March 3, 2017.

109 Nina Nazarova and Kevin Rothrock "The Lives' of Russia's Sex Workers Today," *Meduza*, February 8, 2019.

salon because of the guarantee of receiving clients every day and the promise of some form of security, though in many cases they are still taken advantage of whether it be sexually or financially.

It is a sad cycle many Russian women cannot escape, and it is something the news and media fails to bring light to. Many people looking from the outside think of prostitution as a dirty and disgusting act that low-lifers and junkies engage in, but they fail to see that prostitution is not an enjoyable activity for the average sex worker. Many of these women don't feel any better about what they're doing than the outsider, but they also have no other choice.

Sex work can pay up to three thousand dollars a month, which is more than double the average salary in Russia.[110] If that means feeding her family and having a place to live, many women will swallow their pride and continue to engage in sex work. Becoming a prostitute means losing the ability to walk around in public comfortably, speak to your children without feeling ashamed, and living a life without constant fear. Prostitutes are often so mistreated they become desensitized to the abuse, and can develop mental illnesses and psychopathic traits over a longer period of time.[111] Though there is no current study on the mental health of Russian prostitutes specifically, researchers in 2017 examined a group

110 Nina Nazarova and Kevin Rothrock "The Lives' of Russia's Sex Workers Today," *Meduza*, February 8, 2019.

111 Marboh Goretti Iaisuklang and Arif Ali, "Psychiatric Morbidity Among Female Commercial Sex Workers," *Indian J Psychiatry* 59, no 4 (2017): 468-470.

of prostitutes in India; they found one-fourth of these women had experienced depressive episodes and over one-fifth had PTSD.[112] The impact of sex work on prostitutes is universal. It malevolently works to destroy their mental health and image. Their work changes the way they view themselves and the way their loved ones view them, and it permanently impacts the way they are viewed in society.

While there are many prostitution hubs and defined areas of sex work in cities, prostitution is still considered a misdemeanor that can result in a fine of two thousand rubles, or a whopping thirty dollars.[113] While most countries criminalize the act of buying, Russia punishes the sex worker, allowing the customer to continue partaking in the practice without taking risk. Because there is no consequence for sex rings, there is also no protection for the prostitutes, either. The government refuses to acknowledge the poverty their people are drowning in, but they do nothing to make the people engaging in these activities feel safer. While the government chooses to remain silent in this issue, some concerned citizens have created organizations that make sex work safer for the prostitute as well as the client. Organizations like "Sex Workers' Rights Advocacy Network" (SWAN), "Steps" in Moscow, and the "New Life" offer free condoms, HIV screening tests, and transportation for prostitutes to receive "free supplies and counseling."[114]

---

112 Ibid.

113 "Nina Nazarova and Kevin Rothrock "The lives' of Russia's Sex Workers Today," *Meduza*, February 8, 2019.

114 Ibid.

No unanimous decision exists when it comes to the legality of prostitution, though many argue it should remain illegal, indisputably. Russian women's set of circumstances call for a different case-in-point, one that is too complex for a simple resolution. The cycle of prostitution is going to be a difficult one to terminate, especially considering the government's level of corruption and the number of venal politicians behind closed doors. Women have been discouraged and shunned from citizens as well as male politicians from joining the parliament and maintaining a stance in Russia's politics. A 2017 study shows that 30 percent of Russians are against women joining politics, and 54 percent do not want a female president.[115] How exactly can we break the cycle if half of the country's citizens are misogynistic?

Simultaneously, while many organizations do exist purely for the safety and benefit of sex workers, no law or committee that ensures the safety of these women exists. Many women are exploited and/or forced into the industry. Because the practice is illegal, there is no way to differentiate between those voluntarily involved in the business and those who are not. Prostitution has become a last resort for many of these women, and with no other safety net or reliable source of income, sex work will undoubtedly continue to rise in the years to come.

---

115 "30% of Russians Are Against Women Participating in Politics," *The Moscow Times*, March 3, 2017.

CHAPTER FIFTEEN

MYTHS THAT RUN AND RUIN A SOCIETY

Myths are social constructs that have a large influence over the way particular groups in a society are viewed, scrutinized, and consequently, treated. While many societies have overcome detrimental myths and evolved their thinking to comply with more modern standards, this unfortunately cannot be applied universally. Some misconceptions have made it particularly difficult for women to be viewed as equal in comparison to men, and continue to minimize a woman's place in society. These are just a few myths that have subjected women to mistreatment in several cultures and societies.

Myth #1: A woman's virginity is sacred, and tampering with it leaves her impure.

Women are not kitchen utensils. Women can choose when they want to have sex without being considered dirty and soiled; how many partners they have has no correlation with their personality, skills, or capabilities. The most detrimental issue with this belief is it extends to the legal system in many countries. Arab countries like Iraq, Syria, Libya, and Algeria rarely act upon rape cases, due to the notion that a woman is impure after she has engaged in intercourse.[116] If the victim is unmarried, she is scrutinized for having sex before marriage. If the victim is married, she is accused of infidelity. What these laws fail to see is that rape is non-consensual. The woman had no choice in the matter. These countries enforce stringent laws on which rape cases receive a trial, and prosecuting a rapist under their justice system is incredibly difficult. Many times, survivors will commit suicide due to the immense backlash and judgment they receive from society and their own family. Simply put, a woman's virginity has more value than her existence.

Myth #2: You can conduct a test on women to see whether they are virgins or not.

The virginity test is absolute bullshit, and there is no real way to determine if a woman is a virgin (unless you ask her, of course). I have discussed this in a previous chapter before but I think it's important to really understand the mechanisms of this faulty "test"—if you can even call it that. In many cases, when conducting this test, the doctor will insert their two fingers into the vagina to see how or if the woman reacts to it. The tightness of her vagina (essentially checking to see if her hymen is still intact) and her general reaction to this

---

116 Mais Haddad, "Victims of Rape and Law: How the Laws of the Arab World Protect Rapists, Not Victims," *Jurist,* May 9, 2017.

unethical practice determines whether or not the woman is a virgin.[117]

It is considered faulty because, many times, a woman's hymen never breaks during or after intercourse. It may remain intact many times after having sex. It's even more common for young girls to tear their hymen during sports or strenuous activities that place pressure on that region of their body. Debunking the virginity test is not the main point I am trying to make by acknowledging this myth—it's the fact we are even testing a woman's virginity in the first place. Rape victims and women in strict patriarchal societies undergo this procedure to either ensure they are telling the truth about their rape or to confirm they did not engage in pre-marital sex. It's a disgusting and invasive attack on a woman's privacy and humanity. Unfortunately, this test was commonly used in many third-world countries on victims who claimed they were raped, until it was recently banned by *most* governments in the Middle East and Asia.[118] Many African countries still practice it today.

Myth #3: Menstruation is a sign of impurity and women on their periods should not participate in "holy" activities.

Unfortunately, no part of womanhood can be left untouched from misogynistic and sexist interpretations. Menstruation is a natural reproductive process *almost* every woman and

---

117 "UN: WHO Condemns Virginity Tests," *Human Rights Watch*, December 1, 2014.

118 Ibid.

girl have to endure for a large part of their life. In many Asian and African countries with more traditional values, women are not allowed to step foot into sacred places or partake in daily rituals when they are on their period. This is still practiced in some parts of India, more particularly by religious and/or old-fashioned families. When a woman is menstruating, she is not allowed to step foot into the temple, touch or read the holy book (Vedas, for example), as it is believed her impurities will obstruct prayers and attract evil spirits in a holy place.[119] In some extreme cases, she may not enter the kitchen or touch certain foods, either, as menstruating is seen as unhygienic.[120] It is a sad and outdated belief that, once again, makes it difficult for women to properly function in their daily lives. The very biology of women in some traditions is viewed as inferior and a detriment to a society, and this unfortunate reality consistently keeps women from pursuing the career and future they want for themselves.

Myth #4: Having sex with a virgin will cure a man's sexually transmitted disease, also known as the virgin-cleansing myth.

I briefly mentioned this belief in the previous chapter, but it's important to learn the history and the reason why so many people believe this method truly works. While this practice is largely done in certain parts of Africa, it originated from

---

119 Suneela Garg & Tanu Anand, "Menstruation Related Myths in India: Strategies for Combating it," *J Family Med Prim Care* 4, no 2, (2015): 184-186.

120 Ibid.

Victorian England in the 1500s, with the rampant outbreak of diseases like syphilis and gonorrhea.[121] While the practice eventually came to halt a few centuries later in Europe, it made its way to countries in Southern Africa. It is estimated at least 15 percent of the sub-Saharan population believes raping a virgin or a woman with a disability (the assumption is made she is sexually inactive) can cure a man with AIDs or HIV.[122] The uneducated population in Africa is incredibly high, and this in part contributes to this horrific practice. To protect African girls from the spread of the disease and the obvious trauma (to say the least) that comes with virgin-cleansing, many organizations are working to spread sex education in the continent, from city dwellers to villagers. While many people engaging in the act are aware of the consequences and severity of rape and have pure malintent, others are not because of a lack of basic education and awareness.

Myth #5: Women are biologically less intelligent than men, and therefore inherently make better homemakers.

It is safe to say this stereotype exists in many societies, and it's an underlying theme that keeps women from being taken seriously in the workplace. Currently, 32 percent of girls are unable to attend primary school in Pakistan.[123] Two-thirds

---

121 Leclerc-Madlala, "On the Virgin Cleansing Myth: Gendered Bodies, AIDS and Ethnomedicine," *African Journal of AIDS Research 1,* no 2 (2002): 87-94.

122 Ibid.

123 "Pakistan: Girls Deprived of Education," *Human Rights Watch,* November 12, 2018.

of girls in Afghanistan do not receive any education at all.[124] Only 11 percent of females in Niger are educated.[125] Poverty levels play a small factor in their lack of education, and this can be proven by their male counterparts, who have a much higher literacy rate.

When it comes to being able to afford to send their children to school, families are more likely to withdraw their daughters from school over their sons, with the belief men will have a greater benefit from a higher education. Girls are just as capable of doing great things as boys, only if they have the same resources to do so. Girls should feel encouraged and safe enough to complete school and pursue their careers. No little girl dreams of staying at home and subduing to her husband's commands. They want to be doctors, teachers, writers, and humanitarians. They want to be able to do the same things as their brothers, fathers, and uncles. They want to have their voice heard, but they can't if a hand is covering their mouth.

***

Myths can be a detriment to not only women, but all of society. A multitude of misconceptions apply to men, people of color, and people belonging to certain cultures and/or ethnicities. Myths are insidious beliefs that have a way of shaping core societal beliefs that may not be questioned for

---

124 "Afghanistan: Girls Struggle for an Education," *Human Rights Watch,* October 17, 2017.

125 "Education," *UNICEF,* accessed May 3, 2020.

generations. While many myths have been "debunked" and disregarded by a society, their impact can be everlasting.

CONCLUSION

———

"Equality is not something that can ever truly be achieved. There is no such thing as equality, it's just a fight that will end up in loss."

My ninth-grade social studies teacher was by no means an optimist, and while he was probably just trying to be brutally honest with his students, he wasn't being a realist, either. We may not achieve equality today, tomorrow, or for years to come, but that does not mean we should stop fighting, learning, and trying. He was right, my teacher, to point out that while we have come far, we are not all treated the same. But to tell young children the concept of equality does not exist, and we're better off surrendering to this harsh "reality," is accepting defeat.

We are in the stage of progression. Society has conditioned us to believe this is it and this is the best it is going to get. We have been tricked into thinking historical developments— women's suffrage, the civil rights movement, the Chicano movement—were the epitome of achievement. Today, we can live side by side as equals. This indoctrination, however, cannot mask the brutal images played on our screen every day. Call it sensationalism or propaganda, but the news cannot alter the plot, only the minor details.

I asked one of my friends what feminism means to her. She told me personally speaking, she understands what it is like for a woman to struggle having her voice heard, at home and at school. She knows what it feels like to be scrutinized and undermined in the business field, and hates that people don't take her as seriously. She understood the ideals and values of feminism; however, she said she was unsure as to whether she proclaimed herself a feminist.

I was genuinely confused that while my friend had her own set of struggles pertaining to the movement, she had a hard time completely siding with it. I've heard her talk about how much the pay gap bothers her and how she can't understand why so many boys in her class make sexist jokes. What I later realized, after talking to many of my friends, both male and female, is they do not truly understand the movement as a whole. When I say the word "movement," I am not talking about mainstream feminism; I am regarding every branch, every group, and every belief within the movement.

My friend does not necessarily have a good connotation of the term "feminism," but considering the way she describes her experiences and her set values, she would be deemed one by definition. She is an example of someone who believes in equal rights but finds the term feminism and its movement is one that doesn't necessarily align with her personal beliefs and values. Regardless, she is not invested in the movement and believes she can do well without it. Many men and women fall into this category, and while it does not make them a bad person or sexist by means, it might just mean we need to do a better job of communicating what feminism really entails. The movement shouldn't be something people can applaud but simultaneously shrug over, and that is why I think it is important for each and every woman to talk about her experiences that coincide with the female identity.

It is common for media to portray the movement in a way that makes all feminists look insane—the media is great at highlighting a small number of extremists in any political affiliation—and make their entire group look like radicals with a militant agenda. FOX news will play a clip of a woman wearing a "pussy hat" at a women's rally and ridicule her to no end, finishing up their bit with the typical, "and this is why feminists are uneducated lunatics" line. It's hard to escape that kind of highlight reel, but speaking our stories is something that can help other women and men view feminism from a different light.

Media is not our only restraint. Many of us are surrounded by family and friends that are so resistant to certain movements we forget to formulate an opinion of our own. Others are surrounded by people so apathetic to political issues they never understand the ramifications of remaining neutral. To remain apolitical (on very selective issues), schools will disregard the majority of social topics and students will never get the chance to be educated on incredibly prevalent matters. Everything I have written in this book, aside from my personal experiences, I learned after coming out of high school and leaving the room I occupied in my parents' house for eighteen years. I read things for school and for my own interest. I read things I disagreed with and things I found comfort in. I read disturbing things I wish I did not have to read, things that made me wonder why we praise the human race when many people have no sense of humanity.

Aside from sharing a very global standpoint of a handful of feminist issues, I hope to spark an interest in every reader to learn more about these matters. These issues may not directly have an impact on you, the reader, but they are directly affecting the world around you, and that should be enough to make you want to care.

Once we accept the notion that change is needed, and we are an integral part in the process, we have the ability to change the lives of billions.

APPENDIX

Introduction

Encyclopaedia Britannica Online. Academic ed. s.v. "Feminism." Accessed on April 28, 2020, https://www.britannica.com/topic/feminism.

Chapter One

Alvar, Oliver G. "The Disproven Theory That Was Used to Justify Racism and Sexism."*Cultura Colectiva.* October 19, 2018. https://culturacolectiva.com/history/phrenology-was-used-to-justify-racism-and-sexism.

Encyclopaedia Britannica Online. Academic ed. s.v, "Phrenology." Accessed on April 28, 2020. https://www.britannica.com/topic/phrenology.

Fine, Cordelia. *Delusions of Gender: The Real Science Behind Sex Differences.* New York City: Norton & Company. 2010.

Krucik, George. "The Effects of Testosterone on the Body." *Health-line*. September 17, 2018. https://www.healthline.com/health/low-testosterone/effects-on-body#1.

Rodrick, Stephen. "All-American Despair," Rolling Stone. May 30, 2019. https://www.rollingstone.com/culture/culture-features/suicide-rate-america-white-men-841576/.

"Testosterone—What it Does and Doesn't Do." *Harvard Health Publishing.* August 29, 2019. https://www.health.harvard.edu/drugs-and-medications/testosterone--what-it-does-and-doesn't-do.

Chapter Two

Deck, Jerica. "Why the Fight for Women's Rights Must Include Women of Color." *GlobalCitizen.* January 25, 2019. https://www.globalcitizen.org/en/content/womens-march- diversity-inclusion/.

Dickerson, J. Debra, "Elizabeth Cady Stanton: Abolitionist, Founding Feminist and (yawn) Hypocrite," *Slate.* July 13, 2011. https://slate.com/human-interest/2011/07/elizabeth-cady-stanton-abolitionist-founding-feminist-and-yawn-hypocrite.html.

Encyclopaedia Britannica Online. Academic ed. s.v, "Seneca Falls Convention." Accessed on May 7, 2020, https://www.britannica.com/event/Seneca-Falls-Convention.

Lumen, "The Second Great Awakening." Accessed on May 7, 2020. https://courses.lumenlearning.com/boundless-ushistory/chapter/the-second-great-awakening/.

Rahatt, Camille. "How Alice Walker Created Womanism—The Movement That Meets Black Women Where Feminism Misses the Mark." *Blavity.* February 4, 2020. https://blavity.com/blavity-original/how-alice-walker-created-womanism-the-movement-that-meets-black-women-where-feminism-misses-the-mark.

Segal, Corrine. "Hundreds of 'I Voted' Stickers Left at Susan B. Anthony's Grave." *PBS.* November 8, 2016. https://www.pbs.org/newshour/politics/hundreds-voted-stickers-left-susan-b-anthonys-grave.

Chapter Three

Green, Nadege. "Black Women on Being Called 'Girl' in the Workplace." *WLRN.* May 15, 2017. https://www.wlrn.org/post/black-women-being-called-girl-workplace#stream/o.

Harwood, Morgan. "Equal Pay for Asian American and Pacific Islander Women." *National Women's Law Center.* March 2019. https://nwlc-ciw49tixgw5lbab.stackpathdns.com/wp-content/uploads/2019/03/Asian-Women-Equal-Pay-3.7.19-v2.pdf.

Lean In. "The Latina Pay Gap by the Numbers." Accessed on May 8, 2020. https://leanin.org/data-about-the-gender-pay-gap-for-latinas.

Mazzei, Patricia. "Miami State Senator Curses at Black Lawmaker—and Refers to Fellow Republicans as 'N****'." *Miami Herald.* April 18, 2017. https://www.miamiherald.com/news/local/community/miami-dade/article145327079.html.

O'Brien, Sarah. "Here's How the Wage Gap Affects Black Women." *CNBC*. August 22, 2019. https://www.cnbc.com/2019/08/22/ heres-how-the-gender-wage-gap-affects-this-minority-group. html.

Pierce, Olga and Rabinowitz, Kate. "'Partisan' Gerrymandering Is Still About Race," *ProPublica*. October 9, 2017. https://www. propublica.org/article/partisan-gerrymandering-is- still-about-race.

Taylor, Jamila, Cristina Novoa, Katie Hamm, and Shilpa Phadke. "Eliminating Racial Disparities in Maternal and Infant Mortality." *Center for American Progress*. May 2, 2019. https://www.americanprogress.org/issues/women/ reports/2019/05/02/469186/eliminating- racial-disparities-ma-ternal-infant-mortality/.

Chapter Four

Benderly, Beryl Lieff. "Rosalind Franklin and the Damage of Gender Harassment." *AAAS*. August 1, 2018. https://www. sciencemag.org/careers/2018/08/rosalind-franklin-and-dam-age-gender-harassment.

Crockett, Emily. "Here Are the Women Who Have Publicly Accused Roger Ailes of Sexual Harassment." *Vox*. August 15, 2016. https://www.vox.com/2016/8/15/12416662/roger-ail-es-fox-sexual-harassment-women-list

Golshan, Tara. "Study Finds 75 Percent of Workplace Harass-ment Victims Experienced Retaliation When They Spoke up." *Vox.* October 15, 2017. https://www.vox.com/identities/2017/10/15/16438750/weinstein-sexual-harassment-facts.

Hanks, Angela, and Danyelle Solomon, and Christian E. Weller. "Systematic Inequality." *Center for American Progress.* February 21, 2018. https://www.americanprogress.org/issues/race/reports/2018/02/21/447051/systematic-inequality/.

Nguyen, Janet. "Men and Women Ask for Pay Raises at the Same Rate—But Men Get Them More Often." *Marketplace.* June 10, 2019. https://www.marketplace.org/2019/06/10/men-and-women-ask-for-pay-raises-at-the-same-rate-but-men-get-them-more-often/.

U.S. Department of Labor. "Family and Medical Leave (FMLA)." Accessed on May 4, 2020. https://www.dol.gov/general/topic/benefits-leave/fmla.

"Women's Earnings: The Pay Gap." *Catalyst.* March 2, 2020. https://www.catalyst.org/research/womens-earnings-the-pay-gap/.

Chapter Five

Anderson, Tre'vell. "4 Latino Stereotypes in TV and Film That Need to Go." *Los Angeles Times.* April 27, 2017. https://www.latimes.com/entertainment/movies/la-et-mn-latino-stereotypes-20170428-htmlstory.html.

Dang, Jacky. "Asian Stereotype of Dragon Lady Rises in *Fantastic Beasts 2.*" *AsAm News.* November 21, 2018. https://asamnews.com/2018/11/21/asian-stereotype-of-dragon-lady-rises-in-fantastic-beasts-2/.

Ono, A. Kent and Vincent N. Pham. *Asian Americans and the Media:* Media and Minorities.Cambridge: Polity, 2009.

Ramirez, Charles Berg. *Latino Images in Film:* Stereotypes, Subversion, Resistance. Austin: University of Texas Press, 2002.

Sharf, Zack. "'Get Out': Jordan Peele Reveals the Real Meaning Behind the Sunken Place." *Indie Wire.* November 30, 2017. https://www.indiewire.com/2017/11/get-out-jordan-peele-explains-sunken-place-meaning-1201902567/.

Chapter Six

Lacapria, Kim. "Brock Turner's Father: 'The Girl Got No Punishment for Being a Slut'." *Snopes.* September 9, 2016. https://www.snopes.com/fact-check/brock-turners-father-no- punishment/.

Chapter Seven

RAIIN. "Campus Sexual Violence: Statistics." Accessed on May 7, 2020. https://www.rainn.org/statistics/campus-sexual-violence.

Chapter Eight

Agencies. "'Hyderabad horror' rape-murder suspects shot dead." *World Asia.* December 6, 2019. https://gulfnews.com/world/asia/india/hyderabad-horror-rape-murder-suspects-shot-dead-1.1575603197424.

Bhardwaj, Shreya. "Protests in Telangana Over Priyanka Reddy Rape-Murder Case." *India Ahead.* December 1, 2019. https://

www.indiaaheadnews.com/south/protests-in-telanga-na-over-priyanka-reddy-rape-murder-case-344916.

Kaur, Harmeet. "So-Called Virginity Tests Are Unreliable, Inva-sive, and Sexist. And Yet They Persist." *CNN*. November 9, 2019. https://www.cnn.com/2019/11/09/health/virginity-tests-de-bunking-trnd/index.html.

Mayabrahma, Roja. "Dr. Priyanka Reddy Case: The Brutal Rape and Murder That Left Entire Nation in Shock." *The Hans India*. November 30, 2019. https://www.thehansindia.com/telangana/dr-priyanka-reddy-case-the-brutal-rape-and-murder-that-left-entire-nation-in-shock-585940.

National Violence Against Women Prevention Research Center. "The Mental Health Impact of Rape." Accessed on May 7, 2020. https://mainweb- v.musc.edu/vawprevention/research/men-talimpact.shtml.

Pandey, Siddhant. "Priyanka Reddy Murder Case: Four Accused Arrested by Hyderabad Police." *News Bytes*. November 20, 2019. https://www.newsbytesapp.com/timeline/India/54546/252368/priyanka-reddy-murder-four-accused-arrested.

Winderl, Amy Marturana. "7 Things People Get Wrong About the Hymen." *Self*. October 26, 2016. https://www.self.com/story/the-hymen-what-people-get-wrong.

Chapter Nine

Baruah, Bipasha and Aisha Siddika. "Acid Attacks Are on the Rise and Toxic Masculinity Is the Cause." *The Conversation*. August

13, 2017. https://theconversation.com/acid-attacks-are-on- the-rise-and-toxic-masculinity-is-the-cause-82115.

Chakrabarti, Paromita. "I Feared the Sight of Me Would Scare Her... All She Did Was Snuggle up, and Go to Sleep: Acid Attack Survivor Laxmi," *The Indian Express.* November 22, 2015. https://indianexpress.com/article/india/india-news-india/i-feared-the-sight-of-me-would- scare-her-all-she-did-was-snuggle-up-and-go-to-sleep-says-laxmi-agarwal/.

Chaudhary, Neha. "Acid Attack Survivor Laxmi Agarwal: 'After First Two Surgeries, I Thought I Would Look Prettier Than Before'." *Entertainment Times.* April 11, 2019. https://timesofindia.indiatimes.com/entertainment/events/jaipur/acid-attack-survivor-laxmi- agarwal-after-first-two-surgeries-i-thought-i-would-look-prettier-than before/articleshow/68797628.cms.

Kedia, Shruti. "Laxmi Agarwal's Story and How This Acid Attack Survivor Has Not Just Inspired Deepika Padukone, But Millions of Other Indians." *SocialStory.* June 17, 2019. https://yourstory.com/socialstory/2019/06/acid-attack-survivor-laxmi-agarwal-deepika-padukone.

Commit2Change. "Our Impact." Accessed on April 29, 2020. https://www.commit2change.org/our-impact.

Chapter Ten

Girls Not Brides. "About Child Marriages." Accessed on April 29, 2020. https://www.girlsnotbrides.org/about-child-marriage/.

Girls Not Brides. "Iran—Child Marriage Around the World." Accessed on April 29, 2020. https://www.girlsnotbrides.org/child-marriage/iran/.

Inaya, Naila. "Muslim Conservatives Defend Practice of Child Brides in Pakistan as 'Tenets of Islam'." *The Washington Times.* August 29, 2019. https://www.washingtontimes.com/news/2019/aug/29/child-brides-pakistan-defended- muslim-conservative/.

Nasrullah, Muazzam, Rubeena Zakar, Muhammad Zakria, Safdar Abbas, Rabia Safdar, Mahwish Shaukat and Alexander Kramer, "Knowledge and Attitude Towards Child Marriage Practice Among Women Married as Children." *BMC Public Health.* 14, no. 1148 (November 2014): 2-7. http://doi.org/10.1186/1471-2458-14-1148.

Olson, Carol. "16 Organisations Working to Stop Child Marriage." *The Pixel Project.* December 6, 2013. https://16days.thepixel-project.net/16-organisations-working-to-stop-child-marriage/.

You're a Girl in Pakistan, What Are Your Chances of Going to School?" *ABC News.*October 7, 2013. https://abcnews.go.com/International/girl-pakistan-chances- school/story?id=20475108.

Chapter Eleven

Bar'el, Zvi. "It's Not Easy to Be a Muslim Lesbian." *Haaretz.* June 24, 2018. https://www.haaretz.com/middle-east-news/.premium-it-s-not-easy-to-be-a-muslim-lesbian-1.6201536.

Bilancetti, Ilaria. "The Hidden Existence of Female Homosexuality in Islam." *Jura Gentium.* 2011. https://www.juragentium.org/topics/islam/mw/en/bilancet.htm.

Bilefsky, Dan. "Soul-Searching in Turkey After a Gay Man Is Killed." *The New York Times.* November 25, 2009. https://www.nytimes.com/2009/11/26/world/europe/26turkey.html.

Birch, Nicholas. "Was Ahmet Yildiz the Victim of Turkey's First Gay Honour Killing?" *Independent.* July 19, 2008. https://www.independent.co.uk/news/world/europe/was-ahmet- yildiz-the-victim-of-turkeys-first-gay-honour-killing-871822.html.

Burke, Daniel. "In a Survey of American Muslims, 0% Identified as Lesbian or Gay. Here's the Story Behind That Statistic." *CNN.* May 28, 2019. https://www.cnn.com/2019/05/28/us/lgbt-muslims-pride-progress/index.html.

Emery, David. "What Is Sharia Law?" *Snopes.* June 19, 2017. https://www.snopes.com/news/2017/06/19/what-is-sharia-law/.

Human Dignity Trust. "Map of Countries That Criminalise LGBT People." Accessed on April 30, 2020. https://www.humandignitytrust.org/lgbt-the-law/map-of-criminalisation/.

Labi, Nadya. "The Kingdom in the Closet." *The Atlantic.* May 2007. https://www.theatlantic.com/magazine/archive/2007/05/the-kingdom-in-the-closet/305774/.

Nabbout, Mariam. "Kuwaiti Academic 'Found Cure for Homosexuality.' But it's Not a Disease." *Step Feed.* April 26, 2019. https://

stepfeed.com/kuwaiti-academic-found-cure-for-homosexuality-but-it-s-not-a-disease-2301

Chapter Twelve

Boseley, Sarah. "10 Million Girl Fetuses Aborted in India." *The Guardian.* January 8, 2006. https://www.theguardian.com/world/2006/jan/09/india.sarahboseley.

Cameron, Lisa. "China's One-Child Policy: Effects on the Sex Ratio and Crime." *Institute for Family Studies.* December 19, 2019. https://ifstudies.org/blog/chinas-one-child-policy-effects-on-the-sex-ratio-and-crime.

Invisible Girl Project. "What We Do." Accessed on May 1, 2020. https://invisiblegirlproject.org/what-we-do/.

Robinson, Julian. "Hundreds of Dead Newborn Girls Have Been Found Dumped in Garbage Piles in Pakistan Over the Last Year as Cultural Preference for Boys Drives More Parents to Murder Babies." *Daily Mail.* May 1, 2018. https://www.dailymail.co.uk/news/article-5678025/Hundreds-dead-newborn-girls-dumped-garbage-piles-Pakistan-year.html.

The Pixel Project. "Violence Against Women." Accessed on May 1, 2020. https://www.thepixelproject.net/vaw-facts/.

Chapter Thirteen

"10 Facts About Girls' Education in South Africa." The Borgen Project. Accessed on May 25, 2020. https://borgenproject.org/facts-about-girls-education-in-south-africa/.

Africa Educational Trust. "Girls and Women." Accessed on May 1, 2020. https://africaeducationaltrust.org/girls-and-women/.

Education International. "Southern Africa: Young Female Education Unionists Will Strive for Quality Education for All." Accessed on May 1, 2020. https://www.ei-ie.org/en/detail/15956/southern-africa-young-female-education-unionists-will-strive-for- quality-education-for-all.#gsc.tab=0

History. "Apartheid in South Africa: Laws, End & Facts." Accessed on May 1, 2020. https://www.history.com/topics/africa/apartheid.

Leclerc-Madlala, Suzanne. "On the Virgin Cleansing Myth: Gendered Bodies, AIDS and Ethnomedicine." *African Journal of AIDS Research* 1, no. 2, (June 2018): 87-95. https://doi.org/10.2989/16085906.2002.9626548.

South African History Online. "Afrikaner." Accessed on May 1, 2020. https://www.sahistory.org.za/article/afrikaner.

South African History Online. "Eudy Simelane." Accessed on May 1, 2020. https://www.sahistory.org.za/people/eudy-simelane.

South African History Online. "History of Women's Struggle in South Africa." Accessed on May 25, 2020. https://www.sahistory.org.za/article/history-womens-struggle-south-africa.

The Borgen Project. "10 Facts About Girls' Education in South Africa." Accessed on May 1, 2020. https://borgenproject.org/facts-about-girls-education-in-south-africa/.

Thompsell, Angela. "Racial Classification Under Apartheid." *ThoughtCo.* September 1, 2018. https://www.thoughtco.com/racial-classification-under-apartheid-43430.

UNESCO. "Leading SDG 4 - Education 2030." Accessed on May 1, 2020. https://en.unesco.org/themes/education2030-sdg4.

World Population Review. "Rape Statistics by Country 2020." Accessed on May 1, 2020. https://worldpopulationreview.com/countries/rape-statistics-by-country/.

Chapter Fourteen

"30% of Russians Are Against Women Participating in Politics," *The Moscow Times.* March 3, 2017. https://www.themoscow-times.com/2017/03/03/30-of-russians-against-women-in- pol-itics-a57323

Elena, "Divorce Statistics in Russia." *Elena's Models.* November 29, 2018. https://blogs.elenasmodels.com/en/divorce-statis-tics-in-russia/.

Engel, Barbara Alpern. "St. Petersburg Prostitutes in the Late Nine-teenth Century: A Personal and Social Profile." *The Russian Review.* 48, no. 1 (1989): 21-44. http://doi.org/10.2307/130252.

Globe, Paul A. "Russia Now Has More Prostitutes Than Doc-tors, Farmers, and Firemen Combined" and Other Neglected Russian Stories." *Euromaidan Press.* August 20, 2017. http://euromaidenpress.com/2017/08/20/Russia-now-has-more-pros-titutes-than-doctors-farmers-and-firemen-combined-and-oth-er-neglected-russian-stories-euromaidan-press/.

Iaisuklang, Marboh Goretti and Arif Ali. "Psychiatric Morbidity Among Female Commercial Sex Workers." *Indian J Psychiatry.* 59, no 4, (2017): 468-470. http://doi.org/10.4103.

Nazarova, Nina and Kevin Rothrock "The Lives' of Russia's Sex Workers Today." *Meduza.* February 8, 2019. https://meduza. io/en/feature/2019/02/09/the-life-of-russia-s-modern-day-sex-workers.

"Women in Russia Earn Significantly Less Than Their Male Counterparts." *The Moscow Time.* September 15, 2017. https://www. themoscowtimes.com/2017/09/15/women-in-russia-earn-much-less-than-men-a58950.

Chapter Fifteen

"Afghanistan: Girls Struggle for an Education." *Human Rights Watch.* October 17, 2017. https://www.hrw.org/news/2017/10/17/afghanistan-girls-struggle-education.

Garg, Suneela Garg and Tanu Anand. "Menstruation Related Myths in India: Strategies for Combating it." *J Family Med Prim Care* 4, no. 2 (2015): 184-186. http:.//doi.org/10.4103/2249-4863.154627.

Haddad, Mais. "Victims of Rape and Law: How the Laws of the Arab World Protect Rapists, Not Victims." *Jurist.* May 9, 2017. https://www.jurist.org/commentary/2017/05/mais-haddad-arab-world-laws-protect-the-rapist-not-the-victim/.

Leclerc-Madlala, Suzanne. "On the Virgin Cleansing Myth: Gendered Bodies, AIDS and Ethnomedicine." *African Journal of*

AIDS Research 1, no. 2 (2002): 87-94. http://doi.org/10.2989/16
085906.2002.9626548.

"Pakistan: Girls Deprived of Education." *Human Rights Watch.*
November 12, 2018. https://www.hrw.org/news/2018/11/12/
pakistan-girls-deprived-education.

UNICEF. "Education." Accessed on May 3, 2020. https://www.
unicef.org/education.

"UN: WHO Condemns Virginity Tests." *Human Rights Watch.*
December 1, 2014. https://www.hrw.org/news/2014/12/01/
un-who-condemns-virginity-tests.

ACKNOWLEDGMENTS

———

I would like to thank my family and friends (you know who you are) for seeing my potential when I wasn't able to.

This book would not be nearly as impactful if it weren't for my interviewees. Thank you for sharing your stories, I hope I brought them justice.

Thank you, Eric Koester and New Degree Press, for giving me the opportunity to turn my words into pages.

***

A massive thank you to everyone who showed support before getting to see the book in its final product.

Ryan Milbauer   Sanjana Ojha

Caelan Sujet   Suruchi Narang

Suhas Murthy   Shweta Chandekar

Sohum Patel

Naveen Garg

Juhi Vyas

Arnav Gulati

Neha Jacob

Lindsay Sugay

Rahul Khatti

Irem Erdogan

Rebecca Farinaccio

Sunita Gulati

Marissa Kaplan

Sanjeev Gulati

Neha Narang

Michael Landolfa

Madhuri Bhuyan

Emily Carvalheiro

Sharmila Sherikar

Supriya Narang

Sanjeev Badhwar

Andres Torres Hernandez

Abha Narang

Sudershan Gulati

Ghanisham Das Gulati

Angelica Piccini

Amya Gulati

Kaylee Chan

Gabriela Toscano

Krishna Patel

Eric Koester

Jovelle Melgar

Gulshan Mirg

Krishna Narang

Rajeev Gulati

Jil Modi

Nishika Bagchi

Reeva Paluri

Gauri Deshpande

Sahitya Gande

Sanjay Gupta

Alexa Hnath

Jillian Milano

Selena Gonzalez

Sarah Fattah

Meghna Mahajan

Manjula Khanna

Becky Liu

Sameeksha Meel

Sanjay Deshpande

Grace Wilcox

Sanjana Mandapati

Sabrina Fiordaliso

Kirtana Madiraju

Yashaswi Parikh

Sanjana Belthur

Uday Seth

Swati Singhania

Anshu Saboo

Made in the USA
Middletown, DE
03 August 2021